An Academic's Guide to Social Media

Are you an academic who struggles to know what to post on social media and how to disseminate your research effectively on different social media platforms?

Social media serves as a powerful communication tool, yet while most academics are aware of the benefits of social media, many are unsure of what to post, and how to do it in a way that is authentic, engaging, and above all, comfortable! This user-friendly practical guide is designed for all academics who aim to engage in social media platforms in an effective and productive way. This book explains how academics can build their reputation, develop networks, and disseminate their research. It includes 365 useful post prompts applicable to all mainstream social media platforms which help guide academics on what to post on the platforms they choose to engage with.

The book is designed for all academics at all levels and can be applied across various social media platforms including Facebook, LinkedIn, Twitter, and Instagram.

Kelly-Ann Allen, PhD, FAPS, is an associate professor and Educational and Developmental Psychologist in the School of Educational Psychology and Counselling, Faculty of Education, Monash University and an Honorary Principal Fellow at the Centre for Wellbeing Science, University of Melbourne.

Shane R. Jimerson, PhD, NCSP, is a professor at the University of California, Santa Barbara in the Department of Counseling, Clinical, and School Psychology.

Daniel S. Quintana, PhD, is a psychological scientist at the Department of Psychology at the University of Oslo, and the Norwegian Centre of Expertise for Neurodevelopmental Disorders and Hypersomnias at Oslo University Hospital.

Lara McKinley is an award-winning content producer and social media manager at the Faculty of Education, Monash University.

An Academic's Guide to Social Media

Learn, Engage, and Belong

Kelly-Ann Allen, Shane R. Jimerson, Daniel S. Quintana, and Lara McKinley

Routledge
Taylor & Francis Group

LONDON AND NEW YORK

Cover image: Artwork by Emma Cleine

First published 2023
by Routledge
4 Park Square, Milton Park, Abingdon, Oxon OX14 4RN

and by Routledge
605 Third Avenue, New York, NY 10158

Routledge is an imprint of the Taylor & Francis Group, an informa business

© 2023 Kelly-Ann Allen, Shane R. Jimerson, Daniel S. Quintana, and Lara McKinley

British Library Cataloguing-in-Publication Data
A catalogue record for this book is available from the British Library

Library of Congress Cataloging-in-Publication Data
Names: Allen, Kelly-Ann (Educational psychologist), author. | Jimerson, Shane R., author. | Quintana, Daniel S., author. | McKinley, Lara, author.
Title: An academic's guide to social media : learn, engage, and belong / Kelly-Ann Allen, Shane Jimerson, Daniel Quintana, Lara McKinley.
Description: Abingdon, Oxon ; New York, NY : Routledge, 2023. | Includes bibliographical references and index. | Identifiers: LCCN 2022021931 (print) | LCCN 2022021932 (ebook) | ISBN 9781032056159 (hardback) | ISBN 9781032056142 (paperback) | ISBN 9781003198369 (ebook)
Subjects: LCSH: Social media in education. | Social media--Study and teaching.
Classification: LCC LB1044.87 .A454 2023 (print) | LCC LB1044.87 (ebook) | DDC 378.1/7344678--dc23/eng/20220713
LC record available at https://lccn.loc.gov/2022021931
LC ebook record available at https://lccn.loc.gov/2022021932

ISBN: 978-1-032-05615-9 (hbk)
ISBN: 978-1-032-05614-2 (pbk)
ISBN: 978-1-003-19836-9 (ebk)

DOI: 10.4324/9781003198369

Typeset in Bembo
by SPi Technologies India Pvt Ltd (Straive)

Contents

Preface

The authors of this book (Kelly, Shane, Daniel, and Lara) do not profess to be experts in social media use although the four of us have each conducted research and training in this space (i.e., Allen et al., 2014; Parry et al., 2021; Quintana & Doan, 2016; Ryan et al., 2017). One thing we do have is lived experience on a variety of platforms with different levels of success over time. While we each have different levels of competencies and engagement on social media, each of us use it enthusiastically in a regular fashion, both as ourselves, and contributing to organizational accounts.

As regular social media users, we have seen it used as a catalyst for change, to create community, and most importantly, to put research into the hands of people who can use it.

Social media has impacted our careers and professional learning. We have met new collaborators and embarked on new research projects. And once, one of us even composed a draft of a brief article to *Nature* with a colleague via DMs (direct messages) on Twitter (although it was rejected!).

We weren't always social media fans, but we are now. It is these experiences, paired with our knowledge of the demonstrated benefits of social media for academics, that have guided us to prepare the book that you are reading today.

What is social media?

Social media includes online platforms that enable people to interact and communicate with each other. Through these virtual networks, social media facilitates the creation and sharing of content, thoughts, and information.

Social media is a term that in a modern sense doesn't always fit its traditional definition.

While social media was originally devised as a way to interact and keep connected with friends and family, the modern-day uses of social media have transcended its original purpose, and it is now used in a variety of ways with relevancy and utility for academics. It is not just *social* media anymore, it has become for many the *only* media they consume.

Academics have an important role in this space to ensure that they provide a credible and ethical voice and a source of reliable information in an age of great misinformation, especially on the internet.

This book presents guidelines for academics drawn from research and informed by a group of authors who are navigating various social media platforms in their professional lives every day. We have designed this book to assist academics to communicate scholarly work in a productive and time-efficient fashion.

We recognize that, for academics, *time* is one of our most precious resources. This book aims to help academics to be strategic and smart in how they navigate social media and harness its immense benefits.

While we acknowledge, in Chapter 1, several drawbacks for academics to be aware of, we also highlight the many advantages of using social media. It can be an important part of the traditional research output cycle and lead to dissemination, citations, and impact – especially when the intended audience of your research is also the audience of your social media platform.

Chapters 2, 3, and 5 provide detailed ways in which academics can create a social media presence with ease and flexibility. Chapter 4 specifically provides 365 social media content and engagement prompts with inspiration for creating engaging posts and maintaining a presence. Chapter 6 identifies some of the toxic challenges that may emerge when using social media and provides some ideas and resources to help prepare for them.

We encourage all readers to join us on the hashtag #SocialAcademics, especially if using the 365 social media content and engagement prompts. If you are using Twitter or Instagram, you might like to use the prompts as a social media challenge (e.g., where you draw from the prompts daily; feel free to use the hashtag #365DayChallenge). We hope you can join us to create an engaging and safe community around science communication and academic work.

Chapter 7 presents a collection of ethical considerations which we believe could be readily translated into social media policy or guidelines for academics working in academic institutions.

We believe, as discussed in Chapter 8, that social media is an imperative part of the future of academia and we hope that this book will fill an important gap in the resources currently available. Because of the advantages around impact and citation rates of social media, we believe that all academics should have some basic knowledge and skills in navigating the various platforms available to them. We hope this book will help guide you in discovering both existing and new ways of engaging with and using social media platforms to your advantage.

Best wishes,
Kelly, Shane, Daniel, and Lara

Connect with us!
@drkellyallen @DrJ_ucsb @dsquintana
@Lara_McKinley_ & @SocialAcademics

Acknowledgements

The authors would like to express great gratitude towards the generosity and kindness of Emma Cleine who provided the original cover art for *An Academic's Guide to Social Media*. The painting is called "Bridge" and we feel it is an apt depiction of the connections our readers may make after reading this book to learn, engage, and belong.

We are also thankful to Jonathan Reardon, founder and content creator of @ AcademicChatter, for providing an ongoing source of support and inspiration to us, both as authors, and also to his growing community of academics on Twitter.

Special thanks to Dr. Nicholas Gamble and Dr. Zoe Morris of the School of Educational Psychology and Counselling, Faculty of Education, Monash University for their assistance in the preparation of Chapter 7, *Ethical Standards for Social Media Use by Academics*. Their critical review of the chapter and their expertise in this area is very appreciated and we hope that institutions globally will make excellent use of these standards in policy and practice.

We would also like to acknowledge the contributions of the academics profiled in the book. They were selected because of their proficient and innovative use of social media platforms. Specifically, we would like to thank Dr. Saeed Pahlevan Sharif, Taylor's University; Aida Hurem, Griffith University; Laureate Professor Marilyn Fleer, Monash University; Dr Paul Harrison, Deakin University; Lara Tate, Monash University; Dr. Troy Heffernan, La Trobe University; Dr. Gemma Sharp, Monash University, Professor Nicole Rinehart, Monash University, and Samran Daneshfar, Monash University. We would also like to thank the Twitter users who provided thoughtful and inspiring quotes at the start of each chapter: @ AcademicMarcusJ, @PShannonBaker, @cwalterswrite, @herazhar, @GoatsLive, @KeianaMayfield, @katherinebassil, @ImamPhd, and @JonathanDunnett.

We would like to extend our thanks and acknowledgement to all the university and institutional media teams who equip their researchers and academics with the skills needed to engage in social media. We hope that this book will prove to be a valuable resource. We would particularly like to acknowledge and thank Stephanie Summar, Senior Content Specialist and former Social Media Manager at Monash University whose work encouraging and working with academics to engage on social media has been a catalyst for change.

We would also like to acknowledge our institutions – Monash University, University of California–Santa Barbara, University of Oslo, and Oslo University

Hospital – and Vilija Stephens and Katie Peace of Taylor and Francis for supporting us to undertake this novel project. We hope this book will prove helpful to our colleagues and fellow academics so that they too can use social media safely and productively.

We would also like to thank our families and friends, especially our children who provide ongoing inspiration, perspective, and consultation (Florence, Georgie, Henry, Gavin, Taite, Kayla, Billy, Lily, Noa, and Mila). The older kids already know more than us about social media, and the younger ones will no doubt become more instinctively resourceful and savvy as they grow into a world of online connections and virtual communities.

About the authors

Kelly-Ann Allen, PhD, FAPS, is an Associate Professor and Educational and Developmental Psychologist, in the School of Educational Psychology and Counselling, Faculty of Education, Monash University, and an Honorary Principal Fellow at the Centre for Wellbeing Science, University of Melbourne. She is also the lead co-director and founder of the Global Belonging Collaborative which represents a consortium of belonging researchers and advocates from around the world. Dr. Allen is the Editor-in-Chief of the Educational and Developmental Psychologist and both the current and founding Co-Editor-in-Chief of the Journal of Belonging and Human Connection. Dr. Allen's work is characterized by accessible applications of her research into everyday practice, especially as it relates to the core beneficiaries of the work. The quality of her research has been acknowledged through several awards, including being independently ranked by The *Australian*'s data-science partner, The League of Scholars, as Best in Field for research contributions over the past four years. Dr. Allen's professional standing is verified through her esteemed grade of Fellow for both the Australian Psychological Society and the College of Educational and Developmental Psychologists. You can find Kelly-Ann on Twitter, Instagram, and Facebook @drkellyallen and at her website www. drkellyallen.com.

Shane R. Jimerson, PhD, NCSP, is a professor at the University of California, Santa Barbara in the Department of Counseling, Clinical, and School Psychology. With over 400 publications (including more than 30 books) and more than 350 presentations, he has provided insights regarding; school violence and school safety; school crisis prevention and intervention; developmental pathways of school success and failure; the efficacy of early prevention and intervention programs; school psychology internationally; and developmental psychopathology. His central aim is to bring science to practice to promote the social, cognitive, and academic development of all students. He is currently the Editor-in-Chief of the *School Psychology Review* (NASP) journal and was previously Editor-in-Chief of *School Psychology Quarterly* (APA). He has served as President of the International Association of School Psychologist, Division 16 of the American Psychological Association, and the Society for the Study of

School Psychology. You can find him on Twitter @DrJ_ucsb and on LinkedIn at drshanejimerson.

Daniel S. Quintana, PhD, is a psychological scientist at the Department of Psychology at the University of Oslo, and the Norwegian Centre of Expertise for Neurodevelopmental Disorders and Hypersomnias at Oslo University Hospital. Dr. Quintana's research investigates how hormones and the cardiovascular system influence psychological and somatic health. His research is supported by funding from the Research Council of Norway, Kavli Trust, and the South-Eastern Norway Regional Health Authority. In 2021, he was conferred the Royal Norwegian Society of Sciences and Letters Award for Young Researchers (The I.K. Lykkes Prize) in recognition of his research. Dr. Quintana regularly delivers talks and hands-on workshops on how academics can use social media to boost their careers. He also produces and co-hosts *Everything Hertz*, which is a podcast that discusses research methodology and scientific life in the behavioral sciences. You can find Daniel on Twitter, Instagram, and TikTok @dsquintana.

Lara McKinley is an award-winning content producer and social media manager at the Faculty of Education, Monash University. Lara started her career as a photojournalist, covering stories in Guatemala, Timor-Leste, the United States and Australia and later worked as a visual storyteller in international development. Lara's work has been broadcast nationally and internationally on television, radio, print, and online. She has led social media strategies and built online communities to counter far-right extremism and Islamophobia. Outside her work at Monash, Lara partners with organizations to produce content strategies, visual stories, and story-based content that builds connection, increases engagement and creates change. You can find Lara online on Twitter and LinkedIn and via her website www.laramckinley.com.

Part I
Getting started

1 Social media use in the academy

The positives and pitfalls

The best thing about Twitter is community and seeing that even the bigwigs get rejections and share a dislike of reviewer 2

@AcademicMarcusJ

Introduction

Social media, broadly defined, refers to digital and electronic platforms that support communication and allow content to be created and shared (Cabrera et al., 2017). While there are some criticisms about social media for academics – considered as a distraction from learning, research, and other academic pursuits (Newport, 2019) – for many, social media use is on the rise. In fact, the increased popularity of social media use by academics has spurred a change in the way research is disseminated and engaged with by the general public, other academics, and students.

Academic virtual communities built from platforms like Twitter or work-sanctioned social media platforms like WorkPlace and Yammer have formed and make it increasingly difficult to dissociate social media from what has been traditionally considered academic work.

More specifically, social media use is now recommended for academics by most academic institutions and bodies associated with academic duties (i.e., journals, research groups, professional associations). According to a 2007 study, at least 77% of life scientists were actively involved on social media (van Eperen & Marincola, 2011).

The benefits of social media for academia

Social media has revolutionized the way people communicate with each other and reimagined how professional tasks are performed. Despite a slow integration of social media uptake in the academy, the use of social media has already changed the way academic staff perform their traditional roles and duties (Britton et al., 2019).

Many academics admit that if they want a quick response from a colleague they might contact them on a social media platform, to avoid clogged-up email inboxes. Also, typing takes time. Some social media platforms like WhatsApp, Instagram, and Facebook allow for video and voice recording. After all, alternatives to text can be a clearer and time-effective way to communicate.

Academics use social media for a range of reasons. Social media platforms open communication channels to discuss new project ideas, find new collaborators, or

DOI: 10.4324/9781003198369-2

seek professional advice. Some users have even reported they started writing the foundations of an academic scholarly paper in direct messages (DMs). Social media affords a rapid way to establish communication, even with distant individuals or newly acquainted colleagues (Arshad & Akram, 2018; Britton et al., 2019; Forbes, 2017; Sutherland et al., 2020). In fact, when it comes to interacting with other academics, social media platforms can provide a virtual environment where scholarly communication can take place, such as to discuss manuscripts and the planning of grant proposals. (Britton et al., 2019; Pawlak et al., 2021). These can be either formal (e.g., virtual conferences, meetings) or informal (e.g., Instagram live, Twitter Spaces, or events connected by a hashtag).

Social media has also provided a platform where more senior academics can mentor and nurture the careers of junior scholars as Aida Hurem from the School of Education and Professional Studies, Griffith University describes.

CASE STUDY: Mentors and connections

By Aida Hurem, School of Education and Professional Studies, Griffith University, Brisbane, Australia, (@Will_be_dr on Twitter)

Twitter has been an invaluable tool when it comes to meeting fellow academics and higher degree research (HDR) candidates. For example, through Twitter, I was able to connect with some of my most admired researchers in the field of belonging, such as Dr Kelly-Ann Allen, and others in different areas, who share very similar ontological and epistemological beliefs. In addition to being able to connect with those who share similar research interests, I have also found much benefit in meeting other HDR candidates who are undergoing similar challenges when it comes to the HDR experience. Conversing with them, sharing jokes and memes, has been invaluable in this very long journey, which at times can feel quite overwhelming. Similarly, connecting with more senior academics has, at times, also helped provide some much-needed perspective and even guidance throughout this HDR journey. The academic Twitter community is utterly amazing, and I feel it has enriched my academic experiences.

This benefit of social media has been particularly useful since the emergence of COVID-19. Social media use during lockdowns and isolation periods provided academics with unprecedented flexibility to maintain many of their usual tasks despite these restrictions – especially in regard to networking, connecting with members of the academic community around the world, and building interdisciplinary collaborations without the need for formal meetings via physical forums as is commonly the case (Arshad & Akram, 2018; Britton et al., 2019; Chugh et al., 2021; Forbes, 2017; Pawlak et al., 2021).

For academic parents or caregivers, virtual conferences and professional development opportunities on platforms like Twitter and Clubhouse have been inclusive and flexible enough to allow for more inclusive participation when traditional face-to-face events would have posed a barrier. As the lead author (Kelly-Ann Allen) of this book reflects:

> *When my children were young, I was invited to various locations to offer keynotes at conferences. Within the space of only a few weeks, I went overseas and interstate without them, and I am sure I heightened the separation anxiety of both of my children. Shortly after, I put the brakes on travelling without them – they came to various locations with me around the world including Morocco, but it wasn't always fun dragging them along to conferences and juggling a professional and parental identity at once. Slowly but surely, I began deferring invitations, and the emergence of COVID was a dream come true for my ability to engage in conferences virtually. But also, for the first time, I could easily participate in more professional development than I had done in recent years. Virtual platforms – for me – offered an inclusive way I could engage with academic pursuits without the parental guilt of neglecting my children.*

In addition to flexible use, social media also provides novel dissemination and communication tools for academics. For example, it is now possible to deliver online lectures professionally (e.g., YouTube) while ensuring that any feedback for assignments is rapidly communicated to students, with these options proving to be extremely useful during temporary on-site closures of some institutions due to the COVID-19 pandemic. With consideration of ethical boundaries (see Chapter 7), online platforms can be an avenue to provide personalized support for students (Ansari & Khan, 2020; Boateng & Amankwaa, 2016; Britton et al., 2019; Chugh et al., 2021; Sutherland et al., 2020).

Dr. Saeed Pahlevan Sharif of Taylor's University Malaysia has won several awards for his innovative teaching using social media. He describes his experience in the case study below.

CASE STUDY: Award-winning efforts

By Dr. Saeed Pahlevan Sharif, Taylor's University Malaysia (@dr.saeedsharif on Instagram)

With the lockdown's enforcement, online learning, which was a complementary approach, was upgraded to the main mode of delivery. Right away, I realised that one of the biggest challenges of online learning is to ensure students concentrate on the academic subject taught.

It is unsurprising that students in online modules are often multitasking with non-academic matters such as browsing on social media more than the face-to-face classes. The instructor and other students' pressure that somehow can limit the 'off-task' browsing during the physical class fades away in online classes. On top of all challenges, engaging the learners in a large class of 300-500 students from various programs with different interests and backgrounds has always been a concern. To tackle the above-mentioned issue, I designed 'Finance Live Show' to achieve the module learning outcomes by delivering the content in an informative, interactive, entertaining, and accessible way.

I fabricated the finance lecture like a 'live TV show' with different professionally made items streaming on students' favourite platform, YouTube, every week during the two-hour lecture. The various items in each episode consist of topic-specific intro videos, lightboard pre-recorded videos, recorded videos in my home studio, live stream chat, and surprise videos, along with gaming and activity platforms such as Slido, kahoot, quizzi etc. On top of all that, having a motto of 'finance is fun', I used to surprise the students with unexpected video items after feeding them some finance concepts: making salad in my kitchen, doing yoga at home, playing a Persian drum, hiking and soaking in the river while I was teaching them finance were among them. During the live class, students could talk to me and each other through the YouTube chatbox. Although I had the option to choose the 'unlisted' streaming which only makes the class visible to my students, I opted for the 'public' option, and the live class was available to the world. Gradually the turn-up number became greater than the students enrolled in the module. Apart from my own and students' family members and friends, we had some external active participants who became constant members of the class. The last item in each class was students' experience and satisfaction evaluation through a short questionnaire. Addressing the students' concerns the week after induces the sense of ownership about the module and makes them realise what their opinion means to us.

There is a large amount of evidence indicating a high level of affective engagement in terms of positive emotional reactions, interest, and attitude towards learning as well as behavioural engagement such as willingness to participate, undertake task management, and also participation in class activities using the Finance Live Show. Students showed a higher level of cognitive engagement by going beyond the basic requirements and welcoming challenges rather than lower-level cognitive engagement that involves rote memory. Actively participating in the activities was the indication of a high level of affective engagement. Each week students were sharing some specific moments of the class in social media tagging me which is an indication for their positive emotional reactions, interest, and attitude towards the Finance Live Show. Another indication for the students' affective and behavioural engagement was using 'my', 'we', 'our', 'us' in their posts/comments on their social media posts. Also, sharing the lecture link with their family members and friends is another indication of students' behavioural engagement.

The impact of the Finance Live Show was beyond the classroom. I used to receive many queries about financial investments/analysis in the real world. Some were inquiring which stock to invest in and which platform to start with. As a lecturer, I found it very motivating to realise this module has penetrated so much in students' mindset that they consider learning it for their future career rather than just passing a compulsory module.

Staying informed

The increasing rates of open-access publishing, pre-print publications, and the use of *research highlights* (brief bullet points that summarize the key findings of a research article) have become popular sources of open-access content to share on social media, especially by academics and scientific journals with Twitter accounts (Thoma et al., 2015). The sharing of such content overcomes the barrier of paywalls. The ability to comment or debate published findings online offers academics the opportunity for post-publication peer review and promotion of their work. Paired with the increasingly higher numbers of academics posting their work online, it is much easier for other academics to stay informed about current research (Johannsson & Selak, 2020; Zientek et al., 2018). Platforms like Academia, Google Scholar, and ResearchGate allow scholars to follow the work of other academics for updates.

At the same time, through social media, freely accessible academic resources are also readily available to help academics with a range of tasks such as academic writing and referencing (Thoma et al., 2015). For example, @OpenAcademics is a Twitter account that regularly posts tips and tools for academic writing and research integrity. Some Twitter accounts have a focus on academic wellbeing and mental health (@AcademicChatter). There are also many individual scholars who share analysis code and more complex explainers regarding specific ways to analyze data that serve as professional development for others (co-author of this book, @dsquintana is a great example of this).

Research translation

At the individual level, social media has become a popular tool for research translation. While most academics are expected to produce research outputs, social media extends this work by allowing increased visibility beyond the pages of an academic journal (Chugh et al., 2021; Duffy & Pooley, 2017; Johannsson & Selak, 2020). Any scholarly output, thought, or activity can also be easily promoted and amplified using social media. Online platforms (e.g., Google Scholar, Research Gate, Academia) designed for academics allow research impact to be tracked in terms of the number of citations and online views (Thoma et al., 2015; Zientek et al., 2018). These metrics are often used in grant applications and promotion forms to demonstrate reach and impact of the research (although the definition of academic impact varies across fields).

Research translation involves taking research discoveries or knowledge and adapting them in a way that can be used in day-to-day practice (Long et al., 2015). Consider for instance the values and processes articulated by Bennet and Bennet (2008) in their book *Knowledge Mobilization in the Social Sciences and Humanities: Moving from Research to Action.* They describe knowledge mobilization as "the process of creating value or a value stream through the creation, assimilation, leveraging, sharing and application of focused knowledge to a bounded community" (p. 17). Simply stated, the term *Knowledge Mobilization* refers to moving available knowledge (research) into active use. The emphasis on process means that Knowledge Mobilization approaches need to consider such factors as the unique situation and the needs of the target stakeholders (e.g., community members). At times, universities have faced criticism about the true value of the research they produce and the possible lack of practical applications. A focus on research translation may be one way to overcome such concerns (Figure 1.1).

How can scholars help to further facilitate the practical application of their research?

It is well known that there is a significant lag time between the reporting of scientific results and their application in day-to-day practice, with some researchers even

Figure 1.1 Research translation is the act of using research findings and knowledge gained through research to inform and advance practice and policy.

Source: Photo by UX Indonesia on Unsplash

reporting a 17-year gap for certain fields (Bauer et al., 2015; Green, 2014). This shortcoming is particularly obvious in health-related fields, with reports citing time and resources as obstacles that prevent the translation of new knowledge into practice (Huang et al., 2018; Maloney et al., 2015; Sandalova et al., 2019). The effectiveness or utility of certain methods or practices is insufficient alone to guarantee its use in an applied sense; therefore, academics must consider different means to encourage the uptake of research findings (Bahadori et al., 2016; Bauer et al., 2015; Bauer & Kirchner, 2020). The use of social media is one such mechanism to facilitate the uptake among relevant professionals, especially when using preprints to accelerate dissemination, which is becoming more common across many research fields and disciplinary areas.

Clear communication

Communicating research through social media platforms can be a valuable tool for academics to share the highlights of their research outcomes with key stakeholders. Practitioners and end-users can stay updated with new information without needing to go to full-length papers, which may be paywalled, and in some cases, filled with technical details or jargon (Maloney et al., 2015). Through social media, people may also find useful ideas or approaches that may be rapidly implemented (Dijkstra et al., 2018; Elliott et al., 2020). For instance, Puljak (2016) pointed out there was a Facebook page of the Croatian Cochrane Branch where content about pregnancy, childbirth, and breastfeeding was provided in plain language to a diverse follower group consisting of laypeople as well as professionals. The information was immediately available to those who could benefit. The rapid sharing of research findings does have drawbacks and risks (Dijkstra et al., 2018), however. The misinformation that rapidly spread during the COVID-19-pandemic (Robinson & Spring, 2020) being an obvious example (see Chapter 8). As such, caution does need to be exercised.

While publications in peer-reviewed journals remain the primary choice for researchers to disseminate research (and often in line with the academic performance standards of the institution they are affiliated with), social media platforms have provided an unprecedented way for research to be disseminated to a wider audience (Dijkstra et al., 2018; Klar et al., 2020, Weiss, 2020). The practice of posting on social media allows for further attention to be drawn to one's research, and it is no longer uncommon for scientific journals to have dedicated social media channels where they signpost newly published articles to their followers (Johannsson & Selak, 2020; Pawlak et al., 2021).

Impact

Research impact, in general, refers to the effect, use, or influence of research findings (Penfield et al., 2014). The Organisation for Economic Cooperation and Development (OECD) defines impact as a research contribution to the economy, society, environment, or culture, beyond an academic output (OECD; 2009). Based on this definition, assessing the impact of research is often a murky and subjective process, dependent on what outcomes are being measured and how use or influence is identified (Holmberg et al., 2019; Penfield et al., 2014). Usually, two types of impact can be distinguished. The first, referred to as the academic impact, is mostly concerned with the content quality of individual research, irrespective of its implications, and tends to be measured in terms of citation counts and use by other academics (Allen, 2019; Chang, 2021; Smith, 2001). In this case, high citation counts are often synonymous with high academic impact, with the aim being either related to personal objectives (e.g., higher rankings, career advancement through promotion, increased h-index) or to advance existing academic knowledge (Merga et al., 2020; Smith, 2001).

On the other hand, social impact considers the social benefits of the research to gauge its significance in respect to change and influence (Holmberg et al., 2019). It is often argued that most research outcomes can eventually be translated into ways that add social value, but this is not the case for all research. Hence, social impact and academic impact are clearly distinct, with the main difference being that social impact extends beyond academia (Fryirs et al., 2019; Penfield et al., 2014). *Here is one example*: The knowledge derived from research on apoptosis (programmed cell death), despite being original, has had little impact on health 30 years following its discovery (Smith, 2001). Yet, research which might be considered less innovative or has fewer implications for future research (e.g., identifying the cost-effectiveness of incontinence pads) could have an immediate impact on society. As a result, publishing highly cited articles or in reputable journals, on its own, is now no longer considered sufficient. In recent years the increasing significance of social impact has become particularly relevant for securing funding (Davison & Bjørn-Andersen, 2019; Fecher & Hebing, 2021; Smit & Hessels, 2021; Smith, 2001) with researchers frequently asked to be accountable for how their work will benefit society, particularly when the funding is drawn from public funding sources (Figure 1.2).

Finally, as mentioned earlier, the advent of social media has afforded an opportunity for some academics to modify their traditional roles to include new ones. There is an increasing demand for academics to conduct research that is of benefit to society, and therefore, online platforms provide the means for communicating research findings not only with the general public but also with important public stakeholders (Britton et al., 2019; Carrigan, 2019; Chugh et al., 2021; Johannsson & Selak, 2020; Jordan & Weller, 2018). While online interactions with the former can be a meaningful way to offer expert advice to people in real-time regarding topics of interest, effective communication with stakeholders is of even great importance especially if they are also potential funders of research projects. Public stakeholder reach also bridges the gap between academia and the public by translating research outcomes into actual applications. Hence, in this case, social media can be a practical tool to continuously keep people informed on research progress and results.

The benefits of social media engagement are numerous and summarized in Table 1.1.

Figure 1.2 Social media use for academics is not always sunshine and rainbows. There are a number of drawbacks and ethical considerations that need careful attention.

Source: Photo by Nathan Dumlao on Unsplash

Table 1.1 Benefits of social media use in the academy

Benefits	Sources
Allows for rapid communication with peers, including distant ones without the need to travel.	Arshad and Akram (2018); Britton et al. (2019); Forbes (2017); Sutherland et al. (2020)
Increases the citations of work that is shared on social media	Finch et al. (2017); Quintana and Doan (2016); Smith et al. (2019)
Creates a platform for the promotion of scholarly activities and career development.	Chugh et al. (2021); Duffy and Pooley (2017)
Caters to the provision of instant up-to-date news of current research and access to literary resources	Johannsson and Selak (2020); Zientek et al. (2018)

(Continued)

Table 1.1 (Continued)

Benefits	Sources
Provides an opportunity to offer or read research highlights that can be quickly screened and debated	Thoma et al. (2015)
Offers increased reach and visibility for research dissemination via sharing research online	Chugh et al. (2021); Duffy and Pooley (2017); Johannsson and Selak (2020)
Allows research impact to be tracked since expected citations or views can be estimated based on the online visibility on social media	Thoma et al. (2015); Zientek et al. (2018)
Allows for the recruitment of staff and students or study participants for research projects	Britton et al. (2019); Fileborn (2015); Gelinas et al. (2017); Sutherland et al. (2020)
Builds interdisciplinary collaborations without the need for formal meetings via physical forums or conferences	Arshad and Akram (2018); Berger (2017); Britton et al. (2019); Chugh et al. (2021); Forbes (2017); Pawlak et al. (2021)
Provides new means for practicing professional activities (e.g., lectures, feedback on assignments, student support, etc.)	Ansari and Khan (2020); Boateng and Amankwaa (2016); Britton et al. (2019); Chugh et al. (2021); Sutherland et al. (2020)
Facilitates meaningful interactions not only with other academics but also the general public or stakeholders on a range of subject matters	Britton et al. (2019); Carrigan (2019); Chugh et al. (2021); Johannsson and Selak (2020); Jordan and Weller (2018)
Provides a virtual environment where academic meetings or conferences may be held (e.g., to discuss the writing of papers, plan grant proposals, institutional decisions, etc.)	Britton et al. (2019); Pawlak et al. (2021)

The double-edged sword

Despite any potential benefits, the use of social media for academic purposes can prove to be a double-edged sword. The most obvious danger is related to misinformation – either through consuming it or contributing to it, even unwittingly. Social media, at times, is a landscape of information of questionable quality where almost anyone can post anything (at least within certain pre-established bounds). There is no universal approach that can assess the reliability and quality of online materials, including scholarly resources (Jordan & Weller, 2018; Thoma et al., 2015). As such, there is a risk for academics to discover poor-quality research or information and share it (Dijkstra et al., 2018; Johannsson & Selak, 2020; Lupton, 2014). It can be particularly problematic if unreliable or erroneous information receives "likes" or further distribution (i.e., through sharing). Likes and reshares attach a perception of value to the post, or to the information it represents, and may be more likely to be considered trustworthy.

Reputational risks

Another risk for academics relates to their own reputation. Academics, as human beings, at times can be fallible and flawed, driven by emotion, and may engage with content without necessarily considering the full risks and consequences. Academics can easily comment on posts representing sensitive issues or express their opinions on highly controversial topics. A poorly written statement can cause lifelong damage to an academic's reputation (van Eperen & Marincola, 2011; Johannsson & Selak, 2020; Lupton, 2014). Through social media platforms, academics are exposed to different types of content, and as individuals with their own personal opinions, they might be inclined to post certain comments or even share content which could be viewed as offensive or inappropriate to others within academia and the general public (Johannsson & Selak, 2020). The expulsion of a faculty member from York University for antisemitic posts is a classic example of such a situation that is known to not only lead to reputational damages but also more severe consequences such as the loss of employment (Miller, 2016).

Closely related to the above is the experience of what has been called *milkshake duck*, a popular term that originates from a Twitter meme used to refer to someone who gains positive popularity on social media before being found to have a questionable history (Ryan, 2020). Some academics, being experts in their fields, may engage in discussions via social platforms in order to inform or educate the public on highly technical matters or their experiences (Britton et al., 2019; Carrigan, 2019; Chugh et al., 2021), and as such, they may have many followers while being viewed as highly popular authoritative figures. However, doing so inevitably puts them under the spotlight and at risk of having their online history intensively screened and scrutinized by social media users. The emergence of proof of past misconduct may eventually damage such academics' credibility and cause long-lasting negative impacts on their reputation.

Privacy concerns

Although not limited to academics, the use of social media entails risks to privacy as well. Concerns regarding the likelihood of an account being hacked or personal information being leaked can cause many academics to be reluctant to adopt social media in a professional capacity. One extreme example is that of Dr. Matt Lodder, the director of American Studies at the University of Essex and a senior professor in art history. He had an unexpected experience towards the end of 2017 when a stranger not only plagiarized his scholarly work but also impersonated him.

The person in question had gained a positive reputation in graduate school, but staff and students were unaware that he had been copying the work of Dr. Lodder and stealing biographies and social media posts directly from the profiles of other tattoo experts. There was also a video uncovered where the student presented Dr. Lodder's work (word-for-word) at a conference making his own embellishments but also wearing the same clothing style and tattoos as Dr. Lodder – copied from his own hands! Dr. Lodder's experience makes plagiarism alone feel like a minor concern.

These days we also have rapidly emerging and accessible *deep fake* technologies to consider. While the story of Dr. Lodder may only be the tip of the iceberg, deep fake technology may eventually take things a step further. Many people will already be aware of the account @DeepTomCruise on TikTok which uses artificial intelligence to create short, yet hyper-realistic, clips of the actor Tom Cruise. Such technologies pose new ethical considerations for academics and represent a good example of the need for academic institutions to constantly revisit privacy, ethics, and legal considerations alongside these emerging technologies.

Social media as a time burden

Many universities are actively encouraging academics to have an online presence, which may be perceived as an additional burden on time. The use of social media calls for a need to stay abreast of current technologies, understand privacy policies, and monitor time spent engaging with multiple social media platforms, which can all take time and create an invisible form of labor for academics (Selwyn & Heffernan, 2021; Sutherland et al., 2020; Zientek et al., 2018). In fact, social media use for academic purposes requires a time investment on top of an existing workload already considered by many academics to be unmanageable (Jordan & Weller, 2018; Lupton, 2014; Sutherland et al., 2020). Some institutions place emphasis on the importance of online visibility for academics to disseminate their research and promote the university. Social media use is sometimes included on promotion applications and is considered a notable way to enhance an academic institution's reputation. However, given that academics are often forced to compete for work – either by being securely employed or on probation seeking tenure – the time and skill investment needed for social media use can place an additional burden on people hoping to have success as an academic (Duffy & Pooley, 2017) (Figure 1.3). The drawbacks of social media engagement are briefly summarized in Table 1.2.

Figure 1.3 A gym membership can be good for your health. But attending too little or too much can have negative consequences. And while there are benefits of the gym, like social opportunities, motivation to exercise, etc., there are also drawbacks like smelly equipment and costly membership. Some people go to the gym and others don't. Academics need to navigate social media in the same way and consider the drawbacks and benefits on balance to help make an informed decision as to whether they will use it and how much.

Source: Photo by Jesper Aggergaard on Unsplash

Table 1.2 Drawbacks of social media use in the academy

Drawbacks	Sources
Creates an additional burden of staying up-to-date with current technologies so as not to lag behind.	Sutherland et al. (2020); Zientek et al. (2018)
Identifies that there is a lack of a universal approach that would ensure the reliability and quality of online scholarly resources.	Jordan and Weller (2018); Thoma et al. (2015)
Poses a strong risk of non-reviewed fake news or poor-quality research being picked up, used, and shared by academics due to the content being "liked" by a large number of non-experts.	Dijkstra et al. (2018); Johannsson and Selak (2020); Lupton (2014)
Generates risk of damage to an academic's reputation in case of poorly written comments on sensitive issues or expressing opinions on highly debatable topics.	van Eperen and Marincola (2011); Johannsson and Selak (2020); Lupton (2014)
Requires time investment within a possibly already-packed schedule	Jordan and Weller (2018); Lupton (2014); Sutherland et al. (2020)
Poses risks of content being plagiarized	Jordan and Weller (2018); Sutherland et al. (2020)
Raises privacy concerns	Lupton (2014); Sutherland et al. (2020)
Leads to pressure by universities for academics to be engaged in self-promotion.	Duffy and Pooley (2017)

CASE STUDY: Building belonging while stuck overseas

By Samran Daneshfar, Monash Education PhD researcher

My research focuses on English language learners with a Kurdish background living in my hometown. I was in Iran when the pandemic began and Australia announced its travel restrictions.

The biggest challenge was being thousands of miles away from Monash University. This physical disconnection quickly provoked a mental disconnect as well.

It [was] isolating and, despite everybody's best efforts, the absence of belonging took place. It's very difficult to continue researching when you're not present in the academic context and the time difference between Australia and Iran exacerbated this.

Along with mundane problems, like internet connectivity and a series of rolling electricity cuts, it all added to the burden of remote studying. My ambition to work in academia suddenly felt no longer feasible — staying positive and engaged was tough.

However, I'm a resilient person in the face of challenges. The passion for my research and fostering my future career are big motivators. So, I had to dig deep.

> *I maintained a close connection with my supervisors and we remained loyal friends throughout the whole journey. I engaged with other scholars and their research through LinkedIn and Twitter. This helped me stay in touch and inspired me to continue my journey. I replaced the lack of research assistant and teacher assistant experience with writing. Writing has been a pleasure for me and replaced the lack of academic opportunities I've missed out on being stuck overseas. I'm so happy I managed to survive this roller-coaster journey as Australia's borders finally opened to international students.*

Taking things on balance

There is no doubt that social media has created change in the ways many academics carry out their daily tasks. The increasing demand for academics to adopt social media testifies to the fact that online platforms can positively influence the career growth of academics. However, the drawbacks associated with the use of social media cannot be ignored, and thus, exercising caution when using social media is recommended. Overall, it can be assumed that in our current time the most successful academic would most likely be the one who seamlessly manages to integrate the use of social media into their academic activities without generating more work for themselves. Chapter 2 will describe strategies and tools for making social media use time-effective by identifying your audience and finding the right platform.

2 Choosing your social media platform

> I hear about new pubs [publications], pub calls, workshops, teaching ideas, and more on Twitter. I also can commiserate with others on the ridiculousness and difficulties of academia
>
> @PShannonBaker

Introduction

If you are yet to join a social media site, choosing your platform may not be as straightforward as you imagine. Many social media platforms exist, and for those academics who have yet to explore what options may be available to them to access many of the benefits described in Chapter 1, choosing a platform may feel over-whelming. The trick is to think of social media as something that is serving you, and your career, rather than an extra thing you *should* be doing. There are two key questions to answer before choosing a platform.

1. *What are my career values and goals?*

   One way to reduce feeling overwhelmed is to think about how social media can support your academic career and your research. Getting crystal clear on your values and the goals that flow from them – particularly when it comes to dissemination and impact – steers you not only on which platform to use, but why you would want to use them in the first place?
   Some questions to reflect on:

   - As a researcher, what are your strongest values?
   - What impact do you want your research to have?
   - What goals do you have for your work?
   - How can social media support serve you?

Time and again we have seen social media used by academics for research dissemination, to increase research impact, build and increase collaborations, boost researcher profiles and citations, attract funding, and foster change.
   Having clearly articulated goals and values allows you to be very strategic in how you spend your time and what platform(s) you opt to engage with. It also helps you determine what you will be communicating on those platforms (your key messages), develop a content plan, and decide what content to post.

DOI: 10.4324/9781003198369-3

Figure 2.1 Setting goals and values will help orientate the way you use social media.

Source: Photo by Aron Visuals on Unsplash

It allows you to have a steady and sustainable online presence. It's a kind of muscle memory that you develop, an exercise that gets easier the more you do it (we'll cover the specifics of this in Chapter 5) (Figure 2.1).

2.   *Who do I want to communicate with?*

Based on your answers to the suggested questions regarding your goals and values, you'll already start to have an idea of who you'd like to connect with on social media – your key audiences.

Identifying these people is important as it helps you understand their perspectives, interests, and needs. It allows you to have greater opportunities to connect with them and to determine which social media platforms to prioritize.

Some questions to think about:

- Who are the most important people who need to know about your work?
- Why would they value your work?
- How does your research help them?
- How will they get access to your work?

It's a good idea to be as specific as possible when thinking about these audiences, as it allows you to really drill down and think about where you can find them on social media and what you can offer them in terms of content.

To begin, we often can start quite broadly. 'Teachers' for example is one common response among educational researchers. A series of questions can help you get more defined. What kind of teachers? Primary or secondary? Early career or school leadership? Urban or rural? How are they feeling? Overworked? Overwhelmed? Enthusiastic? Who is the ideal person you want to communicate with? Where can they be found on social media? And finally, why do they care about what you want to say?

From there you can make informed decisions about the time and attention you will dedicate to specific platforms. For example, if your key audience is innovative school principals, it may prove that LinkedIn is a very valuable platform for you, even though it has a smaller number of users compared to Facebook. If you are looking to engage with young, early career teachers, then it could be that Instagram – with the use of some judicious #teachergram hashtags – is a better option. Twitter also can't be overlooked, with a large number of teachers – particularly lead teachers – active on Twitter and in Twitter chats and forming their own communities.

For each key audience that you determine, go through that *drilling-down* process to determine who they are, where they might be present on social media, and why they care about anything you might have to say. There's a real benefit to being on social media because you can take part in conversations that are happening in real time, respond to questions, and flatten academic hierarchies.

Top ten social media platforms

Social media platforms are now widely used by people of all ages for a variety of purposes. Some use them for marketing, entertainment, or academics. The top ten social media platforms worldwide as of 2021 were Facebook, YouTube, WhatsApp, Instagram, TikTok, Snapchat, Reddit, Pinterest, Twitter, and LinkedIn. The following provides more details on what you need to know for each social media app.

Facebook

Facebook (now Meta) allows users to connect with their friends, coworkers, or even strangers for free and is the largest social media platform in the world.

Overview

Facebook's current company's headquarters is located in Menlo Park, California. Dustin Moskovitz and Chris Hughes were Harvard University undergraduates when they established Facebook in 2004 with Mark Zuckerberg and Eduardo Saverin.

Number of users

Facebook has a total of 2.91 billion monthly active users, as recorded in the third quarter of 2021.

Privacy concerns

Facebook has had some incidents that revealed potential gaps in data privacy. If you are using your personal Facebook profile for work (it's the easiest option), you will also need to consider your own privacy settings and level of comfort with the blend of private and work life. An alternative option is to establish a separate page for sharing your work, which is separate from your personal profile.

Usefulness for academics

Researchers can use Facebook to post content, create or participate in groups and create events. American academic Heather Cox Richardson has used it to great effect, posting commentaries – particularly during Trump's administration – giving historical context to contemporary events.

Cost

There are no fees for using Facebook, making it available to everyone. Charges are only applicable to advertisers that market across Facebook. Changes to Facebook's algorithm make it increasingly difficult for organizations to build their reach organically, which means that you may need to pay money if you want your work to be seen by a large audience on Facebook.

YouTube

YouTube is a site that allows users to view and comment on videos.

Overview

In February 2005, three former PayPal employees – Chad Hurley, Steve Chen, and Jawed Karim – founded YouTube, an American online video-sharing platform based in San Bruno, California. Google later purchased the site, making it one of its subsidiaries.

Number of users

As of 2021, YouTube reportedly had 2.3 billion users.

Privacy concerns

YouTube is by default set to public, which implies that anybody may view a user's video. However, settings can be set to private or viewable via a shareable link.

Usefulness for academics

YouTube's Education Channel features a wide range of academic disciplines and topics that viewers can search for. Good use of keywords and longer videos will raise your videos in the algorithm. As YouTube is a part of Google, YouTube videos are featured highly in Google search results, which can boost organic views. Australian academic and adventurer Beau Miles has amassed more than 22M views on his channel, broadly sharing his passion for backyard adventures.

Cost

Although uploading and viewing videos on YouTube is free, viewers may skip the advertising by upgrading to YouTube Premium.

WhatsApp

WhatsApp is a messaging program that enables users to text, talk, and send media to other people or groups.

Overview

After leaving Yahoo! in 2009, Brian Acton and Jan Koum formed WhatsApp. On 24 February 2009, Koum established WhatsApp inc. in California after building the iOS application.

Purpose

In-app text and voice messages and calls on WhatsApp can be made using the internet or a data plan. Files, photos, and videos can also be transferred or shared within the platform.

Number of users

WhatsApp is being used by 2 billion people daily with 100 billion messages sent every day.

Privacy concerns

The user and the people they're conversing with are the only ones who can see the messages and photographs on WhatsApp. Check privacy settings on conversations to see how photographs and videos are being saved on your smartphone.

Usefulness for academics

Students can use WhatsApp to learn and study together using the Group Chat function, as well as send files and audio lessons and for chat. WhatsApp proved particularly useful to break down technological barriers during COVID pandemic, as it offered a low-bandwidth option to stay connected (Blannin et al., 2021).

Cost

No payments or subscriptions are required to use WhatsApp, as it makes use of a phone's built-in data or Wi-Fi connection rather than a mobile plan's voice or text minutes.

Instagram

Instagram is a photo and video-sharing app that allows users to upload and edit images and videos.

Overview

Instagram was developed by Kevin Systrom in 2010. Facebook bought Instagram for $1 billion in cash and equity just before the company's first public offering (IPO) in 2012.

Number of users

As of 2021, the total number of Instagram users was 1.074 billion.

Privacy concerns

Third-party applications, such as those that plan Instagram posts for you, frequently request access to your Instagram data. Users can decide if they will allow another company access to their personal information before permitting them to do so.

Usefulness to academics

Instagram has traditionally had younger users compared to Twitter and Facebook (although this is rapidly changing). The platform can be a good way to reach specific audiences in a visual way. Using hashtags can help make posts more searchable. American Egyptologist Colleen Darnell (@vintage_egyptologist) uses the platform to share her knowledge of archaeology (and vintage fashion) with her 214K audience.

Cost

Using Instagram is free but has been defined in recent years by the presence of influencers who make their living from promoting brands on their platforms. Like Facebook, it hosts advertising.

TikTok

TikTok is a video-sharing app that allows users to upload, share, and discover short videos.

Overview

As the name suggests, the videos on TikTok are intended to be brief. Known as Douyin in China, the firm ByteDance launched it in 2016. TikTok's rise in popularity began in late 2017 with the acquisition of Musical.ly.

Purpose

On TikTok, users can view, share, and upload short videos. Young people utilize the app to express themselves and share interesting facts and fun posts.

Number of users

In 2021, TikTok had about 1 billion active users, which soared from having only 689 million in 2020.

Privacy concerns

In a new section added to TikTok's U.S. privacy policy, the social video app said that it might collect biometric information such as face and voice prints from its content. Privacy concerns may vary country-to-country, depending on where data is stored and who it can be accessed by.

Usefulness for academics

The app's brief video content makes it ideal for enticing someone to view many videos in a short period. A teacher may utilize video creation tools to produce short, customized courses for the classroom and upload them on TikTok for students to view later. Check out Dr. Paul Harrison (@drpaulharrison) who uses TikTok to explain research about human behavior in bite-sized chunks to his nearly 78,000 followers.

Cost

People can download the TikTok app for free. Anyone may use the software to watch videos on TikTok and create their videos on their own personal account.

Snapchat

With Snapchat, users can exchange photographs, messages, and videos, often with filters. These 'snaps' auto-delete once a recipient views them.

Overview

Snapchat was established in 2011 by then-Stanford University undergraduates Evan Spiegel, Reggie Brown, and Bobby Murphy.

Number of users

As of 2021, Snapchat had 96 million daily users in North America and 80 million in Europe. During the most recent reporting period, Snapchat had 306 million daily active users throughout the world.

Privacy concerns

The terms of service for Snapchat state that the company collects information such as a user's name, username, email address, phone number, and birthdate when they access the service. There are also location-tracking settings to be aware of when you set up your account.

Usefulness for academics

Snapchat can teach and relay information using a fun sharing of short lessons or to connect with students in a different way. Professor Jill Walker Rettberg from the University of Bergen used Snapchat stories to share research snippets (Jaakola, 2017).

Cost

Snapchat, in contrast to other social media, does not have a website; therefore, you must download and install the app itself to get started, which you can get for free.

Reddit

Reddit is a resource for keeping up with the latest news or issues and meeting new people with similar interests. Through voting, information and questions are socially selected and promoted by the members.

Overview

Reddit was started by Steve Huffman and Aaron Swartz at the University of Virginia in 2005. The site was purchased by Condé Nast Publications in October of that year. Reddit spun out from Advance Publications, the parent company of Condé Nast, in 2011.

Privacy concerns

Like other social media sites, Reddit gathers information about you and then uses it following its Terms of Service. This includes your email, IP address, and web surfing history, among other things.

Number of users

In June 2021, Reddit had 1.7 billion visitors, making it one of the most popular websites on the internet.

Usefulness to academics

People worldwide contribute to Reddit's educational side by sharing their knowledge and expertise on a wide range of topics. Academia on Reddit (r/academia) is one example of an academic community for sharing academic-related work and issues.

Cost

To utilize most of Reddit's features, you must first register as a member for free. Redditors can pay a monthly or yearly fee to upgrade to Reddit Gold to get access to additional features.

Pinterest

Pinterest is a social curation website that allows users to share and organize photos they find online by creating boards where they can 'pin' things.

Overview

Pinterest was inspired by Tote, an app developed by Ben Silberman and Paul Sciarra that acted as a virtual catalog replacement. In March 2010, Pinterest launched a restricted beta version of the site's prototype.

Privacy concerns

As stated in their policy, Pinterest makes every effort to keep user material and accounts safe. Still, they cannot guarantee that unauthorized third parties won't circumvent its safeguards.

Number of users

As of October 2021, Pinterest had 444 million monthly active users, which ranked it 14th on the list of the world's most 'active' social media networks.

Usefulness to academics

A Pinterest account is also an excellent location to publish supplemental lesson materials, particularly visual content. Users can build many boards and invite specific individuals to join. Professor Inger Mewburn (The Thesis Whisperer) has a brilliantly eclectic and collaborative account (https://www.pinterest.com.au/ thesiswhisperer).

Cost

Individuals and businesses alike can use Pinterest for free. Business accounts have specific promotion and analytics features.

Twitter

Twitter is a social media platform that allows users to post brief messages known as "tweets." This can be text, image, or video-based. Tweets are currently limited to 280 characters. Twitter hashtags have led to movements for change. For example, #blackintheivory was started by Shardé Davis to talk about racism in academia.

Overview

Twitter was founded by Jack Dorsey together with Noah Glass, Biz Stone, and Evan Williams. They all worked together on the project in March of 2006.

Privacy concerns

Even though users can share information with their "followers," the default privacy option on Twitter means that all communications are seen by anybody who signs up for the service.

Number of users

More than 211 million people use Twitter daily, as recorded in the third quarter of 2021.

Usefulness to academics

Twitter is commonly used by academics to network with colleagues, share and obtain information in real time, follow and comment on current issues, and link to industry groups. Some accounts come ready-made with a community such as @openacademics and @academicchatter.

Cost

Creating a Twitter account is free, which enables tweeting and seeing other people's tweets. Users need a working email address or phone number to get started.

LinkedIn

LinkedIn is a web-based and mobile app-based professional networking service. It allows people to connect with coworkers, grow professional networks and search for a job. Posts and articles can also be posted from accounts.

Overview

LinkedIn was established on 5 May 2003, in Mountain View, California. Reid Hoffman and a slew of others, including those responsible for creating PayPal and Socialnet.com, were behind the site's launch. From 2016 until the present, Microsoft has retained ownership of LinkedIn while allowing the company to operate as it is.

Privacy concerns

LinkedIn, by default, may share some information that you may not wish to share. It is important for users to review privacy policies. It may help to view your public profile page for those who are not signed in to LinkedIn.

Number of users

Over 740 million people use LinkedIn in more than 200 countries in the world. In social media circles, it's regarded as a platform with enormous potential.

Usefulness to academics

Beyond using LinkedIn as an online CV, and a place to connect professionally, LinkedIn can be used to recruit research participants, share research findings, post information and updates, connect with industry and for professional development. Organizational psychologist and researcher Dr. Marla Gottschalk has amassed a two-million strong following on LinkedIn and regularly shares ideas, practices and tips for people and companies.

Cost

A free account lets you find and browse other LinkedIn users' profiles and search for people, jobs, companies, and more using search options. Premium features are available.

Working with co-author Lara McKinley in her capacity as a Senior Content Coordinator at Monash Education, Laureate Professor Marilyn Fleer chose to use Twitter as a platform to engage in as described in her case study below (Figure 2.2).

Figure 2.2 There are a number of social media platforms academics can use. Some academics may choose to use a number of them at once.

Source: Photo by Jeremy Bezanger on Unsplash

CASE STUDY: How I joined Twitter

By Laureate Professor Marilyn Fleer, Monash University
  It was a journey, one that started with a big no.
  Being a fossil within the academy, FB [Facebook], Twitter, Instagram, and blogs were all beyond me — or so I thought.

Backtrack 3 years, 3 days, and 3K tweets and you would have heard me respond to being asked to engage in these different platforms with a no, no, no, and no.

Lara … spent three days whilst we were in the field on a shoot convincing me to sign up on Twitter. "It's useful," she said. "Twitter is a great tool for translation of your research," she argued. "You can engage the public, and it can be a powerful recruitment resource for your research," she suggested.

She was right: two years on and I have a following of 3.4K

Being in #Twitterland has brought me into many chat groups, connected me with individuals searching for information, and brought into my hands each day a community in which to share with like-minded people.

The borders between research and the site of their use no longer exist for me. I feel connected with the grassroots of my profession.

The local, national and international spaces are only separated by time zones now. There is no need to be physically present.

But how did this all happen?

Initially what came forward for me was the revelation that I had to have an account and that meant a profile. Lara emailed, "Here are 7 steps to getting your Twitter account set up the right way."

The right way? Imagine doing this on your own. You could wind up with a Twitter handle that you would come to regret.

Each time I tweet, I open up the possibility for someone to check my profile. It is just one click away. How did I wish to present myself? What message did I wish to give? Lara advised "Set up your profile to include your key information and a bit of personality."

But there was more to think about. I had to learn about twitter etiquette. I had to make decisions on how I would respond or how I would present myself on Twitter. What would be my particular twitter persona? Lara advised:

- *Be authentic: Twitter is a place to have a conversation with your colleagues and community*
- *Be a good Twitter citizen: spend some time every day liking, retweeting, commenting on other tweets*

For me it was important to promote the next generation of researchers, and in my field this means women. Twitter could give me the vehicle to do this.

To make this happen Lara said, "Have a good routine with Twitter. Ten minutes first thing in the morning, ten minutes around 5pm to like, retweet, comment."

But what would I tweet about? I needed reassurance. Lara said, "I know some of you are struggling with what to say/cringing/would prefer to stab yourself in your eye with a fork. It's hard. I know. But people follow you for your expertise and what you can bring to them...."

And then there was the professional curation of my Twitter feed. Who did I need to tag? How could quality research be translated in just 280 characters? What content had to be there so that when people looked into my Twitter feed there was something they could connect with?

Our goal was to bring into the Twitter feed content that would be noticed when we launched our Australian Research Council funded programmatic research in 2019.

So what happened? Tweeting each day became an addiction. We brought into our research group a Samoan community who participated in our research. We recruited top-notch PhD students. People who wanted to go further with their own learning. And we used Twitter for our social media campaign to reach out to 3K educators to participate in our national study... with 250 registered before the end of the second day. Twitter worked in just the way Lara had said it would.

What I noticed was that Twitter brought educators into the university and academics into the classroom — as it was happening in real time.

I learned a new language — tagging, social influencers, peeps, hashtags, TweetDeck, direct message (DM), followers, and more.

Research matters. But what matters more is that the results of that research are used where it is needed — in practice. Twitter in 280 characters forces you to distil what matters most, to make it accessible, and to share links that give the detail — plus a photo to help the tweet be noticed.

Life without Twitter would now be like a fish without water. My work has changed forever. If working within an ivory tower to being in #Twitterland is possible for this fossil, then anyone can do it.

What social media platforms are specifically aimed at academics?

In addition to general social media apps, there are certain platforms that are specifically geared towards researchers and academics; these include platforms like ResearchGate and Academia.edu. Sometimes Google Scholar and ORCID are included in this category; however, these sites function more as a repository of a scholar's work, although Google Scholar does have the provision to follow other scholars and receive updates on their work (also receive updates of published materials based on designated keywords i.e., Scholar Alerts).

ResearchGate

ResearchGate is used by academics and researchers to follow other researchers and be alerted when new articles are published.

Overview

Researchers Dr. Ijad Madisch, Dr. Sören Hofmayer, and Horst Fickenscher launched ResearchGate in 2008 with the help of two virologists and a computer scientist. Initially based out of Boston, the company later moved its headquarters to Berlin.

Number of users

ResearchGate claims to have 15 million users and can put you in touch with a large number of academics.

Privacy concerns

The privacy of a ResearchGate user can be protected and only allowed with access if agreed upon. A user is automatically enabled to be shown publicly upon signing up but that can be adjusted shortly after.

Usefulness to academics

ResearchGate is an online professional network where scholars can share and access scientific information and communicate with others, although engagement varies according to the field you are in. Academics can post papers, send messages, and exchange ideas.

Cost

Scientists and researchers may access and share their work for free through ResearchGate.

Academia.edu

Academia.edu is a database and platform for sharing academic research, based in the United States.

Overview

Richard Price started Academia.edu in September 2008 in San Francisco, California. Academia Inc. is its legal name.

Number of users

Academia.edu now has 178 million users and 84,000 monthly users

Privacy concerns

In the United States, it's a legally recognized business that abides by the education industry rules.

Usefulness for academics

Researchers, students, and professionals can look through Academia.edu for academic papers and publicly upload research in the database. Academia.edu allows you to follow academics of interest.

Cost

Scholars and researchers may use Academia.edu for free although a monthly or yearly subscription allows for other features — such as the ability to see who has searched for you online.

ResearchGate and Academia.edu are unique in that they both offer basic networking facilities and are specialized in providing academic-related functionalities such as the collation of citation counts and related metrics (Zientek et al., 2018). Such metrics can be linked to an academic's reputation, and by sharing research content with many people, there is a higher likelihood of boosting one's visibility and citation counts along the way (Weiss, 2020; Zhang & Earp, 2020). These platforms rank academics against each other allowing users to estimate their position in a particular field. Academia.edu will identify if you are in the top percent of scholars and ResearchGate offers RG Score, both of which are regularly used in biographies, promotion and grant applications. It is being projected that a researcher's online presence will eventually be as important as citation counts to evaluate their research impact (Jabeur et al., 2010; Vasquez & Bastidas, 2015). Visibility will be an important consideration for academics in the future.

Personal visibility

Many academics will avoid social media because it feels uncomfortable, too much like self-promotion. Yet, academics routinely engage in self-promotion. The act of applying for tenure, promotion, a leadership position, and a committee role involves presenting activities in the best possible light. Writing a CV, a letter of support, an award application, or a grant application has an element of self-promotion. To succeed as an academic you need to display high scholarly performance in terms of publication metrics, grants and research outputs (Cabrera et al., 2017), but visibility can be also important for building your reputation and profile (Park et al., 2020).

Before social media, personal visibility in academia was primarily built by having publications in prestigious outlets or being asked to give talks at conferences. Social

Figure 2.3 Social media provides opportunities for academics to stand out and be noticed in ways that did not exist before the internet.

Source: Photo by Crispin Jones on Unsplash

media is a new way of building personal visibility that is not subject to the kind of gatekeeping associated with academic journals and conferences. It's how specialized academic social networking sites such as ResearchGate and Academia were created (D'Alessandro et al., 2020; Jordan, 2019) (Figure 2.3).

Building an online reputation and public profile

Building a reputation and public profile is about being known for what you do and what you stand for. It's about being visible. Social media offers an opportunity to reflect your identity and values as a researcher, a leader, and/or a teacher. By having a clear identity, prospective funders and collaborators can understand your research interests and identify your credibility.

For example, when sharing your knowledge with your audience – through plain-English articles, tips, and helpful posts – it is clear that as a researcher you want to put research into the hands of people who can use it.

There are two main ways to build your online reputation and public profile:

1   Curate your biography online

- Use a recent image, professionally shot if possible. It adds to your credibility and builds a connection with the audience
- Use a handle that is logical, searchable, and includes your name.
- Be clear about what you do so others know if they want to follow you, include #hashtags.
- Throw in some personality.
- Use your institutional handle for additional credibility.

2   Getting clear on your message

Being clear and consistent in what you say will help people understand what you stand for. Communications specialist Robert Bray – who has worked with a huge range of organizations and grassroots groups to create change – suggests one way of tackling this is to break up your thinking into three stages: problem, solution, action (Bray, 2000).

It's a methodology that works particularly well if you are an academic who wants people to be able to use and understand your research.

* What is the problem you are trying to solve?
* What is the solution you have found?
* What action do you want your audience to take?

Here's an example from Laureate Professor Marilyn Fleer who researches STEM in early childhood. Her audience is early childhood educators:

* Play is the best way for young children to learn, but it is being pushed aside by curriculum pressures.
* We have developed an evidence-based model to teach STEM based on play.
* Download our free guidelines from our website.

Now it's your turn. Find some pen and paper and see if you can answer the following questions. Limit yourself to one or two sentences and think of who your audiences are.

1   What is the problem you are trying to solve? Why is your work important to your audience? This is the line that will get their attention.
2   What solutions have you found, or are seeking to find? This is a clear description of your research findings or projects
3   What action do you want people (your audience) to take with this information you are offering them? An action can be thinking about an issue in a new way, finding out more, or trying something new.

You can apply this methodology overall to build your personal public profile, but also to your individual research projects. Dr. Gemma Sharp (@gemmasharp11) reflects on her use of Twitter and her journey of developing an online public platform in the case study below.

CASE STUDY: Sharing my voice

By Dr. Gemma Sharp, Monash University
   It may come as a surprise to hear that I was a relative late comer to social media despite being a body image researcher. I had a personal

Facebook profile which I posted on occasionally, but as a researcher, I relied upon my institutional staff webpage to be my online "presence" or "voice."

I was fortunate to be named one of ABC Radio National's Top 5 Under 40 scientists in 2017 and spent two weeks at the ABC studios in Sydney in July 2017. My fellow scientist interns all had Twitter accounts and were quick to praise the benefits of being on Twitter. I think I remember one of them saying "It's like you don't exist if you're not on Twitter." I was initially a little sceptical. I was already short on time, and my university staff webpage was where I spent my time updating my profile. Our mentors at the ABC were also very supportive of us having a Twitter presence, so I caved to pressure in July 2017 and joined Twitter on @gemmasharp11.

Initially I was only really sharing the content of others (retweeting) rather than generating my own content (tweeting). I think I had somehow developed the idea that to tweet it had to be something revolutionary to fill the 140 characters (as was the limit at the time). I considered my TEDx talk in December 2017 on the taboo topic of genital body image to be a pretty big deal so tweeted about that. At the same time, attendees in the live audience at TEDx Brisbane were tweeting brief quotes from my talk. It was at this moment that I realised the power of Twitter and social media and what everyone was trying to tell me during my ABC internship. Social media platforms allow us to distil the essence of our research into highly digestible messages which can be accessed by millions of people around the world. As much as we do not like to admit it, we will never have this many people reading our journal articles or watching our conference talks!

I now had the zeal of a convert when it came to my presence on social media. I did not need to wait for another TEDx talk opportunity to talk about body image. I already had an audience and was part of an online community who were interested in what I had to say, and I them, on a daily basis. The vast majority of my content is focused on body image and eating disorders research and clinical matters which strongly aligns with my offline professional life. I share my own group's research/findings as well as that by other researchers and organisations, so my social media followers know that I will provide them with updates on what I think is important in the field.

While my social media presence is mostly from a professional perspective, I think it is important to still show a more "human" side too. Some of my most popular posts have been about rather mundane but relatable events such as forgetting my glasses and having to lecture in my prescription sunglasses. I am also very partial to a cute animal GIF which always seems to capture the attention of my followers.

It is true that social media does take up time which researchers and academics are already short on. However, you really do get a return on your investment.

Measuring your visibility with altmetrics

Altmetrics are an important consideration for academics hoping to measure visibility and can provide excellent data about the effectiveness of your social strategies. They represent an alternative set of metrics, other than citation-based ones, and measure the extent to which your work is being used. Being a "non-traditional" form of tracking research, it takes into account both the scholarly impact (as listed in standard reference databases) as well as the popularity (based on its presence on social media) of your work.

History of altmetrics

Jason Priem, an information scientist, created the word *altmetrics* in 2010. It initially had the sole purpose of providing a complete record of engagement related to specific academic work, with a focus on engagement and use on social media, print media, and policy.

How does altmetrics work?

The metrics are usually collected from the following platforms:

- Twitter (e.g., how many tweets are about your work and how many users have retweeted it)
- Facebook (e.g., how many times your research has been mentioned publically on walls)
- Wikipedia (e.g., the number of times your research is mentioned)
- Peer review platforms (e.g., Publons)
- Academic databases (e.g., Web of Science citations)
- News, blogs, online magazines, patents, and public documents (e.g., number of views, downloads, comments, reviews, saves, bookmarks, citations, etc.)
- Reference managers (e.g., Mendeley)
- Policy documents

Today the altmetric database contains 189M mentions of over 34M research outputs (including journal articles, datasets, images, white papers, reports, and more) and is constantly growing.

Despite offering a reasonable alternative metric to citation counts alone to address some of the problems around academic vs social impact described in Chapter 1, altmetric scores are often used with some degree of caution over their utility. The pros and cons of altmetric scores are outlined in Table 2.1.

Table 2.1 The pros and cons of using altmetrics

ALTMETRICS	
Pros	*Cons*
• Offers wider coverage than traditional citation metrics • Can be collected faster than traditional citations-based metrics • For researchers, altmetric data may provide an early indication of public attention and visibility. This may be beneficial to early career researchers. • Open access	• Incomplete coverage of use of scholarly work • Being relatively new (since 2011), altmetric data may only cover new sources of information while overlooking older ones. • Reliability of altmetric scores is not easily tracked. • Users hoping to share their work must use the correct link. This is not always the "share" link on journal sites.

Narrowing options

Chapter 2 has presented multiple options for choosing your ideal social media platform and recommended that you first identify your values, goals, and target audiences. For those who have identified Twitter as the platform of most benefit, you may find Chapter 3, *The Twitter Rule Book*, to be highly relevant. Twitter is a preferred platform for many academics, and Chapter 3 will describe why this may be the case.

3   The Twitter rule book

There seems to be an academic urge to use Twitter as a microphone, yet one of its best uses for scholars is as a platform for listening, authentically engaging, and building community.

@cwalterswrite

Your Twitter profile

Consider your Twitter profile like an abstract for a scientific article: it provides a preview for what you're going to tweet. There are a few important elements for your Twitter profile that you will need to consider, which we'll cover below.

Your bio

People will often decide to follow you based on your bio. If you're stuck and not sure what to include in your bio, here's a good template for researchers: [TYPE OF RESEARCHER] researching [RESEARCH AREA] at [INSTITUTION] using [RESEARCH TOOL]. I like to [PERSONAL INTERESTS]. For example, "Psychologist researching biological systems linking psychosocial factors to health at The University of Oslo via genetics. I like to rock climb and drink coffee." Also remember that you can use emojis in your bio, which can add a bit more personality and help you keep under the 160-character bio limit.

Your profile image

While there are various options for your profile image, the most important thing is that you choose *something*. The default Twitter profile image is often associated with bots, so if someone comes across your profile, and it has the default image, they might not choose to interact with you or follow you if they think you might be a bot.

The traditional approach for the profile image is to choose a portrait photo. Some people are fortunate to have a professional portrait photo taken by their institution, which can work well for Twitter profiles. Having the same shot across all available platforms (e.g., an institutional profile page, Google Scholar, ResearchGate) can help boost recognition, but this isn't necessary. Using a photo of your face also helps people recognize you at conferences or in-person events.

DOI: 10.4324/9781003198369-4

But if you are not comfortable using your photo, it's OK. What's most important is that you change the profile image from the default. Some people use a photo of their pets (always a winner on Twitter) or other objects. One example of a popular Twitter account that *doesn't* use a portrait image is that of Daniël Lakens (@lakens), who is an experimental psychologist at Eindhoven University of Technology. When scrolling through a feed, it's very easy to recognize the red square that he uses as the profile image for his account. Coincidently, Daniël chose this red square, which was a visual stimulus as part of an experiment, as it was one of the few images he had on the computer he first set up his Twitter account on.

It's fine to change your profile image from time-to-time, but don't change this *too* often, as people will learn to recognize your profile image and spot it as they're scrolling through their feed. You don't want them to miss your posts.

Header image

The header image is often forgotten, but it's another opportunity to show others what you do and inject some personality into your profile. This image is located at the top of your profile, and it's shown on both desktop and mobile. This image isn't as important as your profile photo, which can pop up in other people's feeds if you're retweeted, as people only see the header image if they visit your profile. Some photo examples include delivering a presentation or your research in action (e.g., fieldwork, archival work, at the lab bench). You could also include a screenshot of a figure from a recent paper or use this to promote any upcoming events. Just keep the recommended image dimensions in mind (1500 × 500 pixels). Twitter also has their own gallery of header images that are the recommended dimensions. There are other websites that you can use with high-quality (and free to use) images, such as Unsplash and Pixabay. If you're looking for a little inspiration or help, there are also several Twitter header templates available on Canva.

Website link

The website link is another opportunity to show people what you do and the kind of things that you will tweet. There are several options for what link you can include here. One of the most obvious websites you can link to is a personal web page or an institutional profile page if you have one. If you have any scholarly publications, you can also include a link to your Google Scholar page. This is a good way to show others your publications, so others can see the kind of research that you do at a glance. Another approach is to include a link to an article or event that you would like to promote. You can include a line in your bio like "See bio link for my latest paper." If you're going to do this, make sure that you link to papers that are not paywalled. It's easy to forget that many of your followers don't have access to paywalled academic journals.

If you can't decide which link to include, several services are emerging that create a simple page with a list of links. One example of this is Linktree, where you create a bio link that will take you to a page with a list of links. These links can direct to any website, but some examples include your Google Scholar page, latest paper, personal web page, or other social media accounts (Figure 3.1).

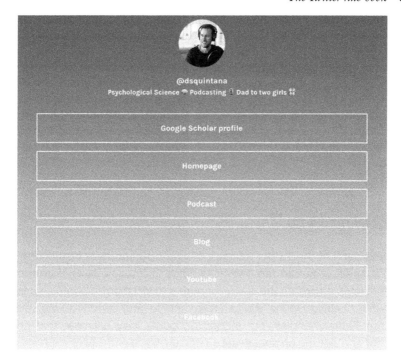

Figure 3.1 An example of a Linktree landing page, which can list several links.

Source: Screen shot by co-author Daniel Quintana

What to tweet

One of the most common uses of Twitter by academics is to share the publication of new articles. While this is certainly an important use, if this is the only time you tweet then you won't be tweeting very often. So what do you do when you're between papers or if you're an early career researcher still working towards your first paper?

You can share your research process. This includes any interesting articles that you're reading, any new research tools you've discovered, and pictures from events you're attending (or screenshots for online events). You might think that other people would find this boring, but what's more boring is not posting anything at all. One way to approach Twitter is to use it as a way to think out loud. By using this "think out loud" approach, you might think that you'll begin to dominate other people's Twitter feeds. But keep in mind that most people follow hundreds of people, so it's very difficult to dominate someone's feed.

Here are a few examples of the types of things you can tweet:

Your own research papers

The most basic form of this tweet is to include the title of your new paper and a link. While this is useful, there are various ways you can increase the chances that others will click on the link or share the link with others via a retweet.

Including an image will help your tweet stand out. You can either take a screenshot of the abstract of your paper so that others can read what your paper is about, or you can include a figure from the paper or the graphical abstract, which some journals offer as an option. Alternatively, you can take a screenshot of a particularly important section of the paper that you think others will find interesting. Of course, you will need to check the license of the paper regarding whether you can share content. If you preprinted your paper, you can share screenshots of text and images from these types of articles as common preprint licenses allow sharing (e.g., CC BY 4.0).

If you have co-authors on your paper that are on Twitter, you can also tag them in your tweet. Also include your institution and department, if they have Twitter accounts.

Social media tip ♀

If you can't fit the Twitter handles of your co-authors or institutions in your tweet, you can tag Twitter handles in images. Note that some users have turned off the ability for others to tag them in photos, so this might not *always* work. You can also reply to your own tweet including these Twitter handles, but tagged accounts may only see the reply tweet and not the original tweet.

Other approaches to increase the engagement of paper announcement tweets include adding a direct quote from your paper or providing a summary of the main points of your paper. Make sure you check out Chapter 4 for more content creation ideas.

Twitter threads to describe papers

Announcing new publications is a popular use of Twitter, but the character limits for individual tweets don't leave much space to describe papers beyond the main points. A solution to this problem is to create a Twitter thread, which is a series of connected tweets. The first tweet of a Twitter thread typically provides a summary of the publication with a link. It also announces its part of a thread by explicitly mentioning it is a thread or including the "thread" emoji (🧵). Alternatively, some people add a "counter" at the end of tweets to denote that this is the first of a series of tweets (e.g., 1/14).

Instead of squeezing as much information as possible into a single tweet, Twitter threads provide some space to better describe a new publication. Like individual tweets, it's useful to add images to tweets to illustrate what you're writing. It can be hard to predict which tweets in a thread will resonate with readers, so try to write tweets that make sense on their own as these are more likely to be retweeted.

Paper threads are popular because they reduce friction and are easy to read. Instead of having to follow a link to a paper in a web browser, Twitter users can get a summary of the paper without leaving the platform.

Hashtags

Hashtags can be a useful way to participate in the various academic communities that exist on Twitter. Adding a hashtag in front of a word, like #this, can make it easier for others to find a given topic of interest. For instance, #AcademicChatter has emerged to be a useful hashtag for Twitter users to discuss life in academia. Popular hashtags tend to be bookmarked by others as saved searches, so it can be a handy way to join a conversation. Hashtags are also a useful way to keep track of discussions at events, like conferences.

> Did you join an event and want to follow what people are posting? Use Tweetdeck or a similar extension service to track the hashtag rather than the search engine here on Twitter. You can keep Tweetdeck in a browser window if you need another tab open
> **P. Shannon-Baker** – @PShannonBaker

Stick to a core theme

People will be attracted to a consistent theme. Of course, it's fine to share tweets that are "off theme" from time-to-time, but having a general theme will help followers keep engaged. Related to this, you should post what you want to be known for, not what you *think* people will like. Only posting memes might help gain followers, and that's fine if that's what you want to be known for. However, if you really want to use Twitter to share your work, very few of your followers will be interested in your actual research if they're only following you for the memes.

Learn by doing

The best way to discover the kind of tweets that receive engagement is to try different things. It's likely that most of these rules and conventions will change over time. Some of the best ways to discover what works is to observe what others are doing and try these things yourself. Twitter includes an analytics feature for each tweet where you can see how many times a tweet has been viewed and the number of times that a link has been clicked.

Participate

Unless you're already well known, it can be very difficult for your tweets to get attention unless you participate in Twitter. The minimum level of participation is to "like" tweets, so that's a good place to start. Beyond this, you can retweet, which shares others' tweets so that your followers can see them. You can also "Quote retweet" which lets you add a comment above the retweeted tweet. In addition, you can reply to other people's tweets.

Including images

Twitter allows you to attach one to four images per tweet. A small preview of these images will be shown with each tweet, but users can click on each image to take a closer look. This is a nice feature if you're including a particularly detailed image (e.g., a screenshot of text). Keep in mind that some parts of your image might be cropped in the tweet preview. Twitter takes a guess on what part of the image to show in the preview via an automated process, but sometimes it can get this wrong. This means that if there's a part of an image that you really want others to see, crop your image so that this key part of the image is around the middle of the image. Regardless, others can see the whole image if they select it.

As most tweets are text, tweets with images stand out, especially when people are quickly scrolling through their feeds. Images are also very useful for sharing a lot more information than you can from text alone, as Dr. David Reilly notes.

> **You can say more with a well designed infographic, or even just a screenshot of your published article title and abstract, than you ever could in 280 characters.**
>
> **Dr. David Reilly** – @davidreillycom

If you're looking for a high-quality image to complement one of your tweets, you can use Unsplash and Pixabay (as mentioned above). For instance, if you sharing a tweet discussing community, using "community" as a search term in Unsplash returns about 2000 images, like this one (Figure 3.2).

Image descriptions

When you add an image to a tweet, Twitter provides the opportunity to add a written description. This is also known as alt-text. This makes your images accessible to those who are visually impaired. If you're sharing a screenshot of a paper caption, you can simply paste in the text of the abstract.

Figure 3.2 This image was found on Unsplash.com, which houses free high-resolution images that can be used for free, with or without attribution.

Source: Photo by Priscilla Du Preez on Unsplash

Adding captions to videos

People who don't use Twitter with the sound on are likely to skip videos if they can't hear what people are saying. Adding captions to videos can increase engagement and accessibility for those who are hearing impaired. There are various services that automatically caption videos and provide the opportunity to edit these captions, such as Headliner. You can also add subtitles by uploading a .SRT file via Twitter Media Studio.

Repurpose your work

A lot of the work you're already doing as an academic can be easily repurposed to share on Twitter. For example, you can record your next virtual presentation, post the full video on another platform (e.g., YouTube or Open Science Framework), and then share a 30 second preview of the video on Twitter with a link to the full video (the current length limit is 2 minutes and 20 seconds). You can also post a link to your presentation slides. Open Science Framework is a good place to host your academic outputs because it's free and guaranteed to be around for at least the next few decades. Importantly, you can associate your work with a digital object identifier (DOI), which makes your output easier to cite.

Don't stress about the details

While Twitter is useful for professional networking, it's meant to be fun. Just look at Twitter's own account (@twitter), which is mainly just tweets making fun of itself. Don't worry if your tweets have minor typos, these things happen and won't limit the reach of your tweets. Of course, if you notice a typo immediately after you send a tweet you can delete it and reshare the corrected tweet. But keep in mind that if you don't get the chance to delete your tweet before someone has replied to or quote retweeted it, others will see that you deleted a tweet. If there have been no replies or quote retweets of a tweet and it has been deleted, there will be no history of this tweet unless it has been archived on a platform like the Wayback Machine (https://web.archive.org/).

Use the search function

Twitter has an underappreciated search function that orders results by relevance and in chronological order. This is a great way to see how people are discussing your research topic and to find interesting people to follow. You can also use the search function to find people who include your search term in their bio or username. This is one reason why it's useful to include your research topic in your bio so that others can find you. You can also combine usernames and topics, which can help you find when a specific user included a tweet with a specific keyword. For example, searching "@dsquintana meta-analysis" will return every tweet from @ dsquintana that included the term "meta-analysis." You can also search for links, which can be useful for checking if others are sharing a specific research article or news story. You can also search for terms within your Direct Messages, which can be very useful if you're a heavy Direct Message user.

Build a network of smart, funny, interesting people who talk about things in your space. Search for topics, follow the people with something to say. Follow the people that reply, follow the people they follow.

Colin Simpson – @gamerlearner

Your goal shouldn't be to make all your tweets go viral

When you're looking through your timeline, you'll probably come across a lot of tweets that have received impressive retweet numbers. It's easy to think that *everyone else* is posting viral tweets, but you're only seeing these tweets *because* they've gone viral. If you were to click on the profile behind the viral tweet, it's likely that most of their other tweets haven't got much engagement. It's also very difficult to predict which tweets will go viral because there's a lot of luck involved, such as who happens to see the tweet.

Tweeting on behalf of groups and organizations

While the dominant use of Twitter is by individuals, it's common for accounts to be set up on behalf of groups and organizations. For instance, most universities now have a Twitter account where they share news and highlights. Setting up an account for a research group is a useful way to give group members experience with Twitter, as you can rotate curators from week to week. To denote who's tweeting, these group accounts often provide a brief introduction of the curator at the start of the week and the name and Twitter account of the curator is included in the account bio.

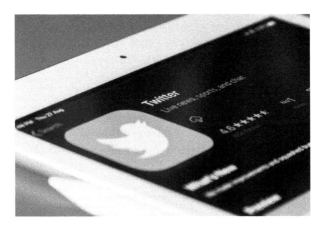

Figure 3.3 Twitter has many benefits for academics, but there are a number of rules and considerations that academics should be aware of.

Source: Photo by Souvik Banerjee on Unsplash

CASE STUDY: Using social media to promote a journal or research group

By Dr. Shane Jimerson, University of California Santa Barbara (@DrJ_ucsb on Twitter)

With the leadership of one of the authors (Dr. Shane Jimerson), who is Editor of School Psychology Review (SPR), *this journal team began developing a social media plan in 2019, which launched across multiple social media platforms in 2020. Twitter (@SchoolPsycRev) and Facebook (@SchoolPsychReview) were the initial social media platforms that were piloted, as it was evident the target audience were most active across these two platforms; however, the Journal has expanded to YouTube and Instagram.*

It can be difficult to predict which platforms will yield the most engagement, so by trying a number of different platforms, SPR was able to evaluate which platforms generated the most engagement. After sharing content on these four platforms, SPR discovered that Instagram posts only returned a low level of engagement, so the team stopped posting on Instagram so that they could better focus on the other three platforms. Of these platforms, SPR found the highest level of engagement on Twitter, with over 7600 followers as of March 2022.

While most Journal twitter accounts simply share a title and link to new papers, SPR's Social Media team uses graphics to enhance interest in new articles, shares video summaries of research, ask questions to the SPR audience, and post news articles of interest to the SPR audience. The SPR Social Media team also periodically expresses gratitude to members of the editorial team, by including a picture and link to their online bio. Canva is used to create images for posts (e.g., celebrating holidays, SPR anniversaries, highlighting national School Psychology Week).

The SPR Social Media team is led by the SPR Social Media Manager (calendar year appointment, with possible extension), which is a volunteer position. The main tasks of the SPR Social Media Manager are to regularly post on and monitor four social media accounts (Twitter, Facebook, Instagram, and YouTube), in collaboration with the SPR Editor. The SPR Social Media team (members determined by invitation of the Editor) provide support and consultation to the SPR Social Media Manager.

The SPR Social Media team uses multiple tools (e.g., Altmetrics, Impressions, Engagements, Likes, Retweets, etc.) to monitor the engagement of their audience. This allows the team to adapt their strategy as needed based on metrics.

While these examples are specific for a journal, these are also applicable for large research groups that regularly share new research.

What to post

At this point of the book, you might be seeking more ideas about what to post. Maintaining a social media presence is a balancing act: a balance between promotion and engagement, between sharing your research and sharing who you are as an academic. Most of all it's about creating content that people want to engage with – and engaging with them. It takes time, and consistency, to build up a following. Coming up with ideas can be tricky, especially if you are feeling vulnerable.

Chapter 4 will give you 365 content and engagement prompts for social media that are designed to be a mix of serious research content as well as relatable human content. Test them out. See what works, try to stay consistent, and most of all try to have some fun.

Part II

Social media content and engagement prompts for busy academics

4 365 social media content and engagement prompts

#SocialAcademics

> As a newbie academic coming from the policy world, I have noticed that there are academics who ONLY post about their work/subject. And then there are those who tweet about other things in their life & I'm much more inclined to follow/interact with them
>
> @herazhar

Introduction

This chapter offers 365 content and engagement prompts that provide ideas for regular posts and also offer suggestions on ways in which academics can engage on social media and build their networks (and following).

Some considerations when using the content and engagement prompts:

1. The frequency of the post and engagement prompts lend themselves better to some platforms over others (e.g., Twitter). However, the ideas can be adapted to other platforms such as LinkedIn, albeit at a slower pace. It's important to think about your key audiences and how you can create content that is meaningful and useful to them.
2. Don't 'post and ghost.' Try to engage, listen and respond to posts and comments by members of your social media community.

The content and engagement prompts are divided into nine themes that represent a variety of ways in which you can engage with your audience. These nine themes include mechanics, research, personal, inspire, academic life, engagement/advice, gratitude, supportive, fun. Mixing up the different ways in which you engage in social media will assist your audience engagement. The themes are explained in Table 4.1.

Let's build our own community

If you use the content and engagement prompts, consider using the hashtag #SocialAcademics to build a community. Follow other accounts that are using the hashtags to find other like-mind academics who are interested in sharing their work on social media and networking. Table 4.2 outlines 365 content and engagement prompts.

DOI: 10.4324/9781003198369-6

Table 4.1 Themes of engagement and content creation

Theme	Meaning
Mechanics	Technical things to consider on social media platforms, as well as housekeeping ideas
Your research	Research papers, research dissemination, research impact, accomplishments, and what you're working on
Personal	Personal content – this helps people connect with you and often generates the most engagement
Inspire	Posts that can inspire people and that reflect on your sources of inspiration
Academic life	Workplace, workplace culture, things that support academic life, relatable content
Engagement/Advice	Asking questions, offering advice, interacting with the audience
Gratitude	Gratitude makes anyone's feed lovely
Supportive	Being a good colleague, collaborator and Twitter citizen
Fun	Random, light-hearted, fun stuff

Table 4.2 365 content and engagement prompts

Idea	Prompt	Theme
1	It's time to check your bio. Is it up-to-date? Does it reflect all that you and your research interests have? Have you tagged the place where you work? **Go a bit extra:** Include something fun at the end that reflects a hobby, sport, or quirk about you.	Mechanics
2	Share a snippet of one of your research findings. If you don't have any yet, share something insightful you have read. **Pro tip:** Who published the work? Make sure you tag them. Oddly, publishers are often neglected in social media posts about published works, but they have a vested interest in promoting your work too. Tag them because they are likely to help amplify your message.	Your research
3	Something about you as a person. Post about what you are doing today, your likes, your dislikes, a funny memory from the week. **Note:** Following someone that posts only about their work can become dry. The community you build will be more engaged if they see you as a person and someone they can relate to.	Personal
4	Share a quote from someone you admire who represents a central concept or theme related to your field, work, or research interests. **Go a bit extra:** Embed your quote in an image by using one of the many free apps available (e.g., Canva).	Inspire
5	Flash back to an instrumental paper in your field that was written more than 10 or 20 years ago. **Go a bit extra:** Find a quote from the paper and share the link to the paper so others can read it, either as a screenshot or text snippet.	Academic life

(Continued)

Table 4.2 (Continued)

Idea	Prompt	Theme
6	Ask a question? Something you have always wondered? Or something you want to know more about? This will help encourage conversation. If you are new to Twitter, why not ask #academictwitter for some tips?	Engagement/Advice
7	Share a photo of a legend in your field, someone who has left a legacy that has informed your work. It might have been your PhD supervisor or advisor, or it might be a great theorist. @SocialAcademics If you have met that person and have a photo, share it!	Gratitude
8	Share something about your core research interests that others usually don't know. Are there common myths or misconceptions? State an interesting fact or two.	Your research
9	Plug a pal. Amplify the work of someone else. Share their research or some good news they have received, an award or promotion. **Note:** Posting about yourself, your book, your paper, or an achievement can feel awkward, and if it is your only content you share, it might drive people away. One way you can get around this is by creating a culture where you celebrate the work of others, and they might give your work a plug too – and if they don't, there is nothing wrong with asking them to do the same for you in a private message.	Supportive
10	Use a GIF to describe how your week has been so far and ask others to do the same.	Fun
11	Follow 10 new people who reflect your research interests and engage with one post each of theirs. **Pro tip:** If there is someone you particularly get a lot out of from following them on Twitter, see who they are following to find other like-minded people.	Mechanics
12	Latest research. Post something hot off the press or give a shoutout to some newly published work related to your field. **Go a bit extra:** Visuals improve your content so include a picture of your smiling face holding the paper.	Your research
13	Do you have a reading pile of things you want to get to but never have a chance? Or something you hope to read one day? Share a snap or image of your reading goals.	Personal
14	Share a post about what inspires you and where you get your inspiration.	Inspire
15	Share a snap of where you like to work. **Note:** If you are a mid to late-career academic, early career academics and students can find it quite insightful to see the processes around how you work. Do you print your papers? Do you spread your work out over the floor? Do you have a favorite reading chair? How is your desk set up?	Academic life

(Continued)

Table 4.2 (Continued)

Idea	Prompt	Theme
16	Spend 10 minutes today going through your feed and commenting on the posts of your colleagues. **Go a bit extra:** Instead of simply retweeting or sharing content, try to add thoughtful words or insights.	Engagement/Advice
17	Appreciation post. What do you love about your job and what are you grateful for?	Gratitude
18	Show your work in progress. It might be a screenshot of something you are writing or a photo of you at work. Share your goals around what you are trying to achieve.	Your research
19	Who do you work with? Share a post about a team, colleague, mentor, or someone you work with (e.g., What is something about them that is awe inspiring? What are some of their recent achievements or papers? What attributes do you admire?).	Supportive
20	Describe your research using a GIF and ask others to do the same.	Fun
21	Time to review your bio picture. Is it time to update it? **Go a little deeper:** Book in to get professional photos taken. Some institutions offer this service for free for staff.	Mechanics
22	Share something about your core research interests that others might find useful or surprising.	Your research
23	Post the top five books that changed your life. **Go a bit extra:** Tag the authors and publishers on those books. It's possible they have a decent following and may share or retweet your post further amplifying you and your work to a broader audience.	Personal
24	Share your all-time favorite research article and why it inspires you. How has it contributed to your growth as a scholar? Why do you like it? What makes it special?	Inspire
25	What is distinguishing or unique about your workplace? Share a "behind the scenes" photo. Don't forget to tag your workplace if they are on social media.	Academic life
26	What is the favorite tool you use that helps your work? It might be a software or a manual that you use. It might even involve seeking advice regularly from a supervisor or mentor. Ask your community about their favorite tool!	Engagement/Advice
27	Shout out to someone who helps you accomplish your work. This might be a person in your personal life. Acknowledge them and pay gratitude for how they support you.	Gratitude
28	Tell your story. What motivated you to enter a career in academia? **Go a bit extra:** Find a photo of when you first started and compare it to now.	Your research
29	Amplify the work of one of your PhD students or a PhD student whose work you admire.	Supportive
30	Because jokes tend to attract a lot of engagement, share your best joke. Bonus points if it relates to your area of research or to your career in academia. **Go a bit extra:** Use hashtags like #AcademicChatter to amplify reach.	Fun

(*Continued*)

Table 4.2 (Continued)

Idea	Prompt	Theme
31	How do you #hashtag? Review what hashtags you are using in your posts to increase reach and engagement. Including hashtags in tweets can increase engagement. Twitter recommends only using one or two hashtags per tweet. On Instagram, consider putting them into the first comment. **Pro tip:** Do a quick #hashtag search to get an idea of the volume of posts using it.	Mechanics
32	Share something you wrote or created and mention how you came to create it. What process was involved? **Go a bit extra:** Create and share an image of an important quote from the piece.	Your research
33	Share a photo of your pet and describe what it does for your wellbeing. If you don't have a pet, take a photo of a place that helps you feel calm.	Personal
34	Tell your audience about your favorite book and why it's your favorite (e.g., why it motivates, inspires, or makes you think).	Inspire
35	Tell your story. What inspired you to do the research that you do or what first ignited your passion? If you do not do research, think about what inspired you to teach. What drives you?	Academic life
36	Spend 10 minutes today following PhD students at your faculty and engage with 10 of their posts.	Engagement/Advice
37	Thank somebody for an insightful post and how it made you think in a new way.	Gratitude
38	Spotlight your research and describe what the benefits are for your intended audience. Does it shed light on something new? Does it provide something practical like strategies or new ways of thinking? Does it expand the field for other researchers?	Your research
39	Share a quote from a recent article you have read related to your core research that sparked your interest. Remember to tag the author. **Pro tip:** Include a link to the journal article, ideally to a non-paywalled version of the article if available.	Supportive
40	Share a photo you have seen recently that made you smile. This does not have to relate to your core research interest. It is important to include lighter, more personal content, so people can see that there is a person behind the post. You might choose to share your family, kids, or pets, but please be mindful of the public nature of your post. Some academics choose not to put their kids on social media while others carefully take curated photos where faces or other identifiable information are not visible.	Fun
41	Time to review how you have been doing. Jump into your statistics (analytics in Twitter) and see what content has performed well. What has tanked? Does content with imagery perform better?	Mechanics

(*Continued*)

Table 4.2 (Continued)

Idea	Prompt	Theme
42	Do you have any examples of the impact of your work? This might involve reported change that has resulted from your research or feedback about your research that relates to impact. You might have a story to share where your research has made a difference to somebody's life or created something beneficial to an organization.	Your research
43	Retell the time you wrote your first post, article, or book. Tell your audience how the idea came about. **Go a bit extra:** Provide a link or snippet from the piece.	Personal
44	Share a famous quote that represents how you are feeling today.	Inspire
45	Take a photo of your office and share a couple of reasons why this is a favorite space. Mention some of the features in your office that make it a great place to work.	Academic life
46	Share a top tip related to being an academic (i.e., how you succeed, thrive, or cope). Ask your audience for their best advice.	Engagement/Advice
47	Celebrate a great collaboration you are involved with. This post is especially good with a photo of you and the people you are collaborating with.	Supportive
48	Share the silliest picture of you on your camera roll and ask if you are the only one who ends up with photos like this.	Fun
49	When do you post your content? Are you posting at peak times, when people are online and receptive to your message? Spend a few minutes reviewing this. **Pro tip:** Use Tweet Deck and other social scheduling platforms to post content at times when your audience is most likely to be online. Some even give you this information.	Mechanics
50	Describe your research area and why it is needed. What problem is it addressing?	Your research
51	Celebrate a win. What is something that went well for you recently and how did it make you feel?	Personal
52	Celebrate a loss. Working in academia is not always about successes. Sometimes we might lose out on a much-wanted award or grant. A paper might be rejected from a desired journal. Share how you cope, what you will do next, or what you learnt.	Inspire
53	Share some fun facts about your work.	Academic life
54	Share a top tip related to your work, research, or teaching. Think about what your audience might be interested in learning from you (e.g., how to interact with industry, how to review a journal article, how to engage in service).	Engagement/Advice
55	Ever receive helpful feedback? It might be a nice email from a colleague or student or perhaps a positive teaching evaluation. With permission, share a quote with how it makes you feel. How does positive feedback shift workplace culture?	Gratitude

Table 4.2 (Continued)

Idea	Prompt	Theme
56	Post an interesting fact from a topic relevant to your core research interests.	Your research
57	Celebrate another academic and their achievements.	Supportive
58	Posts that are relatable and have a human element tend to be more popular. Share a funny story that has happened to you in your life.	Fun
59	What image are you using in the header of your profile? It's in a prominent spot. Can you use it more effectively? It could be a photo of you speaking at a conference or something promoting your latest book. It's valuable real estate. Why not use it?	Mechanics
60	Share some type of a case study. This might involve (for the purpose of social media) something really brief. Sometimes people might use a before-and-after photo, if that is at all possible. The goal is to share a short story or post about a change that occurred from your research.	Your research
61	Share a post that starts off with "When I was a child, I wanted to be…"	Personal
62	Share a story from work that will make people feel gushy and heart-warmed.	Inspire
63	Share a snippet of your day in a behind the scenes kind of way, no matter how boring it may seem at that time. **Go a bit extra:** Attach a photo.	Academic life
64	Ask your audience a question. Some examples would be what you do to unwind, what you like most about academic work, and what is your biggest goal this year. Or you might choose to relate it to your own research interest.	Engagement/Advice
65	Share a list of three things you are grateful for in life. Ask your followers to share their list with you in the comments.	Gratitude
66	Share a recommendation for a resource that is related to your core research interest. This might be an article, book, podcast, or event. It doesn't have to be your work; it could be the work of somebody else.	Your research
67	Share a book chapter that you read recently that you found interesting. Pro tip: Tag the author.	Supportive
68	Share your favorite meme, preferably something that relates to academia or your core research interest. **Go a bit extra:** Create your own meme. There are various websites that allow you to do this (Canva, Imgflip, Filmora, Wondershare PixStudio, Quickmeme, Meme Generator, Imgur, Make a Meme, Livememe, ILoveIMG, Meme Creator, DIYLOL, etc.).	Fun
69	Try your hand at a different kind of storytelling today by doing a Tweet thread. It's a great way to outline the key findings in a research paper, for example. Number the tweets so people can easily follow along. **Go a bit extra:** Consider the images that you post with each part of your thread.	Mechanics

(*Continued*)

Table 4.2 (Continued)

Idea	Prompt	Theme
70	List three ways you hope your research findings can be used by others.	Your research
71	Share how you relax when you're not working. If you have a picture that's a bonus.	Personal
72	Share a handwritten inspirational message for your audience.	Inspire
73	Use this post as an opportunity to share good news where you were recently cited by someone or featured somewhere important. Did you win an award? Sometimes these posts can make us feel a little bit awkward, but often people prefer you to be upfront with your accomplishments as opposed to being sneaky with them (humble-brag).	Academic life
74	Do a "how-to" post related to your core research interest.	Engagement/Advice
75	Share a picture of you with your parents and talk about how they helped you in becoming what you are today.	Gratitude
76	List the top five questions that you receive related to your research. You might collect these questions from conferences, classes you teach, or workshops you run.	Your research
77	Following on from the previous post, what are some of the responses to those questions? You might choose to break these posts into five separate posts with the question and the answer.	Supportive
78	Post your 'current mood' in GIF form.	Fun
79	Share a great post with a thoughtful comment about why this content is valuable. Not only does this support a colleague, it also shares your expertise with your community.	Mechanics
80	Update your staff profile page with a summary of your work and journal articles and share it. It's a good opportunity for people who can't access journal articles to know what is there.	Your research
81	Share a picture of your kids, spouse, or pet and talk about their significance in your life, if you feel comfortable sharing this information.	Personal
82	What is something that you thought was impossible that has come to fruition?	Inspire
83	Share a highlight of the year from an event you have attended. **Pro tip:** Take candid photos at events, including one of signage. They come in handy not only to thank the organizers but also for all kinds of future content.	Academic life
84	Share a recent purchase that makes your academic life easier. Think of a new book or stationery or a comfortable new chair. Are you the only one who gets a thrill of delight from this?	Engagement/Advice
85	Give a shoutout to your mentors and the people who have supported you to get you where you are.	Gratitude

(*Continued*)

Table 4.2 (Continued)

Idea	Prompt	Theme
86	Do you have a conference, workshop, or talk coming up? This is an opportunity to post about where people might be able to find you to come and have a chat if they are around or to promote attendance at one of these events.	Your research
87	Shout out or mention someone you admire most.	Supportive
88	Share your favorite song that relates to your core research interest or a song that comes to mind when you think about your research interest. Most artists post their songs on YouTube, which are easily accessible. Not everyone may have access to the music streaming service you use.	Fun
89	Follow your top 20 journals, and commit to engaging with them regularly **Pro tip:** Make a Twitter list of your top journals, so you can actively follow and engage with their feeds.	Mechanics
90	Demonstrate in a post how much time is involved in the work you do so that people can truly appreciate it. For example, you might talk about a journal article you have just finished and provide a link. Talk about roughly how long it took you to create that research. Sometimes there are years involved in creating an article and sometimes it can be under review for a lengthy period.	Your research
91	Share a glimpse into family time during the weekend.	Personal
92	Create a post that talks about days when you don't feel motivated, or you are simply having a bad day, and describe what you do to overcome those feelings. This might involve acknowledging other people and their role in supporting your wellbeing.	Inspire
93	Ask your audience a question that relates to the experience of being an academic. For example: what do you think about the high rates of rejection in research articles? Or how you think the peer-reviewed process can be improved. Remember to respond.	Engagement/Advice
94	Share something you have noticed about your audience. You might create a post that celebrates how many new followers or subscribers you have. You might share a thought around how wonderful it is to have a community that you have built or supporters you can draw from. Share a thought that acknowledges your audience and shows them gratitude.	Gratitude
95	Is there a short clip, YouTube link, or even a short movie that describes your research or is related to your research? Use this post to share a link to something that describes your research.	Your research
96	Use this post to describe your research collaborations. This could be colleagues you work with overseas or interstate. You might use this as an opportunity to highlight their research.	Supportive

(Continued)

Table 4.2 (Continued)

Idea	Prompt	Theme
97	What's something you struggled with this week? Post a relatable meme.	Fun
98	How can you get more visual with your content? Research shows that visual posts (photos and videos) consistently attract more reach and engagement. **Pro tip:** If your photos are looking a little fuzzy on your smartphone, try cleaning the lens.	Mechanics
99	Create a free Open Science Framework account, post your most recent presentation slides, and then share the link. Take a screenshot of four interesting slides and include these as images in the tweet.	Your research
100	Share something from the past about yourself or something you were involved in your current workplace.	Personal
101	Share an inspiring quote by somebody who works in your field.	Inspire
102	Working in academia often involves having multiple tasks and expectations. Some people find that parts of the job intimidating and scary. For instance, some academics do not enjoy public speaking, and they avoid things like conference presentations and meetings. Use this post to describe how you have overcome your fear about something and how it resulted in a positive outcome. How did you grow from the experience?	Academic life
103	Do you keep a to-do list? Use this post to talk about strategies or purchases that are personal to how you maintain an accomplishment or to-do list each day.	Engagement/Advice
104	Reflect on a recent or past award you have won and emphasize what is special or unique about the award. Why is it important? You might start off your post with "Remembering a time I…"	Gratitude
105	Share a news article that relates to your purpose. This might mean sharing an article that presents the problem that your research is trying to address, or it might be an article where you were interviewed or contributed to. Or it might be an article that explains the motivation, reason, or rationale for your research.	Your research
106	Congratulate a PhD student for passing a significant milestone or having a terrific supervisory meeting.	Supportive
107	Share a funny story about something that happened at work.	Fun
108	Set up a Google Scholar account (if you haven't already) and post a link to it. **Note:** Become familiar with Google Scholar, who is citing you, and who is publishing research in your area. Receive topic alerts and ensure you are sharing the latest research regularly.	Mechanics
109	Share a post about something you have done recently or written. Share a link to your research or a grant you have won.	Your research

(*Continued*)

Table 4.2 (Continued)

Idea	Prompt	Theme
110	Share a life lesson. Again, this is an opportunity to embed some humor or find a meme or an image on the internet you could share, or you might want to post something quite serious that you reflect on.	Personal
111	Post a motivational article or quote that could appeal to all academics. Use relevant hashtags or try out #academictwitter and #academicchatter	Inspire
112	Share a behind-the-scenes photo of you working on your computer.	Academic life
113	Share a problem that you are having at the moment. This might be something that you are thinking about and can't resolve. It might be something that's related to your research. Ask your audience what ideas they might have to help solve your problem. This might be a philosophical idea related to your core research interest. You might also use this post as an opportunity to talk about something personal such as a joke related to getting the kids to clean up their mess.	Engagement/Advice
114	Share a story about friendship in your workplace and what it means to you.	Gratitude
115	Introduce somebody new to a social media platform to your audience so they too can receive followers.	Supportive
116	Share a fun fact about working in academia, something that people would not know.	Fun
117	Are you consistently tagging relevant people and organizations in your posts? Not only is it good manners, it's a way of bringing your content to the attention of the people you acknowledge.	Mechanics
118	Share the changes you have made while working on your research.	Your research
119	Share a ritual or tradition that you practice or have coming up. Posting about special occasions like religious holidays, birthdays, New Year's, Valentine's Day, and many more can provide good opportunities for social media content.	Personal
120	Share what inspired you to do a particular research project.	Inspire
121	Share something that explains and shows a common goal in academia. This could be citations you've received this year on Google Scholar or downloads of an article. Use screenshots as a visual. If it feels too 'boasty', lighten it with a GIF.	Academic life
122	Share a post by somebody you deeply admire. Bonus points if they have a large following. Make sure you tag them. **Go a bit extra: Write a thoughtful** comment to go along with the repost.	Engagement/Advice
123	Reward yourself for your biggest accomplishment this month. Share a photo of that.	Gratitude

(Continued)

Table 4.2 (Continued)

Idea	Prompt	Theme
124	How is your research being used in the community? How does it make you feel to see it? Pro tip: Include a photo of you, or your work in action.	Your research
125	Who are the people you work closely with outside of academia? Give them a shoutout, even better with a photo. How do these partnerships make your work possible?	Supportive
126	Share a playlist of the music you listen to while you're working	Fun
127	Time to review how strategic you are with your social presence. Is it serving your career goals? How can you bring it into alignment? It's time to review your three-month plan. **Pro tip:** What are the messages are you trying to convey over time?	Mechanics
128	Find a research paper from a top journal and point out one or two highlights related to the style or technique (perhaps tapping into writing skills). Bonus points if you choose an article related to your interests.	Your research
129	Share something that you love.	Personal
130	Reflect on and remember the most awesome experience of your career today. This is a way to savor a positive memory and show others that they too can savor those positive exciting events that have happened in their lives.	Inspire
131	Share what your parents think about your research (or the subject you research). Your parents might believe you are still researching something that you might have done earlier in your career.	Academic life
132	Academics use a lot of jargon that the general public does not understand. Use this post as an opportunity to refine the constructs related to your core research interest or something related specifically to your field.	Engagement/Advice
133	Share a story about kindness that has occurred in your workplace and the impact it had on workplace culture.	Gratitude
134	Create a tutorial related to your core research interest. This may be brief, and it could be in a series of tweets, or it could be in just one tweet. It could be one strategy or approach, or you may choose to create a short video.	Your research
135	Share a behind-the-scenes photo of you working with your colleagues. It might involve being on an online call.	Supportive
136	Share a picture of something pretty or beautiful, just because.	Fun
137	Who are your key audiences? Are there people and industries that you'd specifically like to reach? Spend some time today following, and interacting with, key people and organizations. **Go a little deeper:** What content can you create that supports or helps those audiences?	Mechanics

(Continued)

Table 4.2 (Continued)

Idea	Prompt	Theme
138	Share a lesson you have learned from your experience working in academia or your experience, knowledge, or expertise in your specific core research interest area.	Your research
139	Share something that you did this week.	Personal
140	What is a piece of art that inspires you and why?	Inspire
141	Have you had a career change related to work or are you working in a different institution or university from when you first started? Use this post to talk about why you changed and what you like about your new work even if it is not necessarily recent.	Academic life
142	Ask your audience if they have any questions about your research, and use that post as an opportunity for a question-and-answer session.	Engagement/Advice
143	Create a post about a political figure who has advocated for or represented your area of research, if applicable. If not, use another person of public interest like a celebrity or academic who has paved the way for your research. **Go a bit extra:** Include their photo and tag them	Gratitude
144	Share random facts about your core research interest.	Your research
145	Share a post that you really enjoyed and you found thought-provoking, and tell your audience that you find the post to be clear and useful.	Supportive
146	Share the number of internet browser tabs you have open right now and challenge others to beat that.	Fun
147	Twitter lists help you be more efficient with your time and strategically engage with your community. Create a Twitter list today of people you want to follow and engage with more strategically. Pro tip: Be careful with what you call your list, as the people you add to it are notified, and it can be seen	Mechanics
148	Is your research based on personal experience? Share a little about this.	Your research
149	Selfie time! Have you ever noticed when you search Google images for a picture of a professor, many of the images that come up will generally be male, especially an older white male, sometimes with a beard? Use this post as an opportunity to take a photo of yourself and share the person behind the post. Note: Usually, pictures of yourself generate a lot of engagement, and your audience will find your social media output easier to relate to if they know where it's coming from.	Personal
150	Has anybody within your research field or area died during the last 12 months? Create a post that celebrates their work and contributions and acknowledges how they have inspired you in some way.	Inspire
151	Share a post related to how you keep a healthy lifestyle. You might share a picture of your healthy lunch or a picture of how you might stay active in between your academic work. Ask others what they do.	Academic life

(*Continued*)

Table 4.2 (Continued)

Idea	Prompt	Theme
152	Share a research hack that makes your work much easier.	Engagement/Advice
153	Share a software tool that you used today in your research. Thank the clever folks who invented it, just to make your life easier.	Gratitude
154	Does your research need to be shared with politicians and policymakers in government departments? Spend some time today following those social accounts.	Your research
155	Share something you are super proud of. This might be something related to your own work or the work of others. Think about the people you mentor or your students and think about things that make you super excited for them that you could share in a post.	Supportive
156	Share something that you find amazing. Start your post with "This is amazing…" Bonus points if you can find a photo and if it's really quirky.	Fun
157	Time to research what Twitter chats might be relevant for you to participate in. It's a great way to connect with people in your relevant industries and also to pick up new followers. **Pro tip:** If you are participating, it's a good idea to warn your followers so they know why you've got a string of tweets coming out.	Mechanics
158	Share three ways that you could address the problem that your research area is trying to respond to.	Your research
159	Do a post that reviews the week, month, or year you have had.	Personal
160	Reflect on an International Day that is coming up. What inspiration can you draw from the theme?	Inspire
161	Share a hot tip about a common problem that can occur within academia and how you avoid it.	Academic life
162	Related to the previous post, share a mistake you have made and how you learned from it. Such a post not only shows the person behind the post but also your vulnerability, which can make you more likable. However, choose your mistake carefully to ensure that it does not disclose anything that may cause legal or personal harm to you or create reputational damage or backlash.	Engagement/Advice
163	Who is somebody in your field who defied traditional ways of thinking to create new knowledge or research pathways? Reflect on that, and send them your thanks.	Gratitude
164	Dust off your design skills in Canva and create a Twitter-ready infographic on soon-to-be-released research. Visuals aren't part of the 280-character limit, and there's an awful lot you can say with a meaty infographic.	Your research
165	Share a tip for graduate research students. Think of something that may have benefited you when you were undertaking your further studies. Start your post with something like "Here's a hack for graduate research students…"	Supportive

(*Continued*)

Table 4.2 (Continued)

Idea	Prompt	Theme
166	What is something that you are so bad at doing it brings joy to others when they witness it? Dancing? Drawing during Pictionary?	Fun
167	Are you checking your notifications regularly? This is where you'll see who has started to follow you, tagged you, and if you have any direct messages. Best to check every time you jump on the platform.	Mechanics
168	Create a GIF of a set of presentation slides (one of the save options in PowerPoint), and share the GIF as a quick preview of this presentation.	Your research
169	Ask me anything (#AMA) can be a good way to prompt engagement from your audience.	Personal
170	Who is a public figure, outside your field, who you admire? Why do you admire them? Is it for their creativity, tenacity, or passion? Reflect on how you can channel this in academic life.	Inspire
171	What are the top three things that you value about your work?	Academic life
172	Share a story about something good that happened in your workplace. It might have been an act of kindness or generosity. Something you experienced or observed.	Gratitude
173	Describe how you protect yourself from interruptions at work and ask people to share their own strategies. **Go a bit extra:** Use humor. Ask your followers to share "wrong answers only" or reply using GIFs.	Engagement/ Advice
174	Share a metaphor or simile that encapsulates something that describes your research area. This could be a bit tricky, so if it is easier, you might want to share a story instead.	Your research
175	Often, institutions release new reports, have new events and celebrations, or perhaps reach some kind of important milestone in terms of rankings or other things that institutions as a whole might prioritize. Use this post as an opportunity to share something special about your institution and why you feel proud to work there. If none of those feelings resonate with you, then use this post as an opportunity to share something about some news of your own or colleagues.	Supportive
176	What was the worst/first job you ever had? If you could time travel, what would you say to your past self?	Fun
177	Time to reflect on the style of your content by putting yourself in the shoes of your audience. Have you got the mix right? Can you inject something fresh into your account this week?	Mechanics
178	Use this post to share one of your older papers, if you have one. It might be a book or chapter or it might be somebody else's. Use the post starter called "Blast from the Past."	Your research
179	Write a thread on a few things you've changed your mind about in the last few years.	Personal

(*Continued*)

Table 4.2 (Continued)

Idea	Prompt	Theme
180	Do you have a secret pleasure that supports your creativity? The smell of a fresh *National Geographic* magazine? Coffee art from your local café? Writing in a red hat? Share one of those tiny pleasures.	Inspire
181	Post your goal for the week. Start your post with "Goal for the week is to …" Here you might add something serious, or you might embed some humor, such as learn how to use TikTok (we have to aspire to something).	Academic life
182	Create a post about something that you thought was completely overwhelming. It might be something that you are doing currently, something you hope to do in the future, or something you have done and actually overcome. **Go a little deeper: Tell the story with a picture or photo and share that.**	Engagement/Advice
183	Write down something that made you laugh recently. Thank the person who caused that laughter.	Gratitude
184	Record your next presentation and then share the audio on your Open Science Framework page. For example, Zoom provides the option to record presentations. You simply need to save the presentation as an audio file. Use Auphonic to clean up the audio (up to two hours of audio cleaning per month is free). Then share the link to the audio.	Your research
185	Create a post that celebrates a recent publication by one of your colleagues. Talk about the potential impacts of the findings.	Supportive
186	Create a "This or That" poll related to work or study.	Fun
187	Your Twitter analytics page shares your most popular tweets per month. Go through this list and retweet (or quote retweet) one of your older tweets that received a lot of engagement at the time. But don't do this too often as some people think retweeting yourself is passé.	Mechanics
188	Share a Wikipedia page that discusses your core research interest or something relevant to your work. In the past, Wikipedia has been considered as not a reliable source of information; however, this is changing. (https://theconversation.com/students-are-told-not-to-use-wikipedia-for-research-but-its-a-trustworthy-source-168834, https://edtechmagazine.com/higher/article/2017/12/wikipedia-trustworthy-academic-resource-scientists-think-so)	Your research
189	Create a post about a highlight of your career. Start off with "Remembering the time…" **Go a bit extra:** Attach a photo. This is an important way of savoring those special memories.	Personal
190	What wisdom do you think we can learn from children, especially as researchers? Answer the question and ask your audience.	Inspire

(*Continued*)

Table 4.2 (Continued)

Idea	Prompt	Theme
191	If it has been a busy week in particular, make this post one that celebrates something you have done to help you unwind. **Go a bit extra:** Take a photo of something that has helped you relax and keep things in perspective this week. It might be a photo from a walk or a picture of the beach or a cup of coffee.	Academic life
192	Have you ever received an awful review or rejection letter from a journal? Use this post to describe a setback and how it made you feel. **Go a little deeper: Include a part of the rejection letter** (removing any identifiable information). Explain to the audience how normal and common rejection letters and setbacks are and how important it is to keep moving forward. Normalizing rejection is important for early career researchers and graduate researchers to understand and see as commonplace so they do not attribute such setbacks to their own competencies. While we might think that there are different things to improve rejection within academia, given the current publication structure we must, for now, find ways to live with that.	Engagement/Advice
193	Do you have an accountability partner or group that supports you? Give them a shoutout for how they help.	Gratitude
194	Spend 10 minutes today to find and pitch an outlet that can publish an article that is a plain language translation of your research.	Your research
195	Share the most recent paper you have read and why it captured your interest. Tag the author, if they are on social media.	Supportive
196	List three things you love about your job or your work, with an associated emoji.	Fun
197	Reset and recalibrate your social media strategy and plans by getting back to basics. What are your career values? How can social media support them? What are your goals over the next three months? **Pro-tip:** Clean up the list of people you follow.	Mechanics
198	Share some personal wins or results.	Your research
199	Create a "day in the life" post. It's another way to look behind the scenes and draw attention to the different elements of your day. **Go a little deeper:** Create a collage representing different time points in your day.	Personal
200	Who is regarded as the founder of your research area? Why is that person inspiring?	Inspire
201	Create a video tour of your workplace. If you're filming other people, make sure to ask them for permission to be recorded. **Go a bit extra:** Experiment with Instagram reels.	Academic life

(Continued)

Table 4.2 (Continued)

Idea	Prompt	Theme
202	What was a piece of advice that has always stayed with you?	Engagement/Advice
203	Is there somebody who was an influential teacher in your life? What long-lasting impact did they have? Write a post reflecting this. **Go a bit extra:** Include a photo of you at the time.	Gratitude
204	Share a statistic that made you laugh or feel surprised. Add a GIF.	Your research
205	Take a screenshot from an interesting passage of a paper you're reading. Also add the link to the paper. Note: If the paper is behind a paywall, have a look to see if a preparing or author-accepted manuscript version is available.	Supportive
206	Create a Twitter poll. This could just be for fun (e.g., Coffee or Tea?) or you can ask more serious questions (e.g., Have you ever appealed a journal editor's decision?). These polls can often lead to interesting conversations.	Fun
207	Who are the main journalists covering your area of research? Can you do 15 minutes of research today and follow them on social media? **Go a little deeper:** When you see them post an article, share it with your take on the story.	Mechanics
208	Remember that pitch you made 10 days ago? Spend some time writing the article today. People who can use your content will thank you.	Your research
209	Share a photo of what you loved doing when you were a child.	Personal
210	What inspired you to become a researcher? What impact did you want to have? Write a post about that.	Inspire
211	Share life hacks for time management.	Academic life
212	Share a question you are asked ALL the time – and answer it yourself. Chances are there might be someone in your audience with the same question who might benefit from your response.	Engagement/Advice
213	Who is somebody in non-academic life who supports your work?	Gratitude
214	How's your plain language article coming along? Ready to post a link to it yet?	Your research
215	Give a shoutout to your local café, or barista, who keeps you sane. Tag the corporate account if they are on socials.	Supportive
216	Share a picture of a random object in your favorite color.	Fun
217	Time for a quick communications audit. Where are you promoting your social accounts? Think about your email signature, any web presence you have, and business cards if they are used in your community.	Mechanics
218	Share the details of a project you are going to start.	Your research

(*Continued*)

Table 4.2 (Continued)

Idea	Prompt	Theme
219	Think of the last thing you did at work that you felt proud of. Was it a promotion, a grant, a publication, or helping a colleague? Keep that thought in your head. What prompted you to do that? Was it being inspired by someone else? Was it a problem you saw that you wanted to change? In this post, describe your motivation towards something you did and then what you did as an outcome.	Personal
220	Where do you get your light bulb moments from? Talk about one that landed recently.	Inspire
221	Make a "stop doing" list and share it.	Academic life
222	Share mindful productivity boosters that work for you. For example, do you use writing strategies or techniques and to-do lists? Ask your audience to share theirs.	Engagement/Advice
223	Create a list of the blogs you keep up with and talk about the topics these blogs cover. Thank the authors.	Gratitude
224	Is there an election coming up this year? Is your research relevant? Spend 10 minutes jotting down ways you could respond to a breaking story.	Your research
225	Do you work with colleagues from other disciplines? Give them a shoutout and say what you've learned by working with them.	Supportive
226	It can be incredibly helpful to follow accounts that are completely outside your area just to watch how the masters of social media do it. Just google 'best corporate accounts on social media' and follow a few that take your fancy. Or just trust us and follow Netflix and KFC. Then share your favorite one.	Fun
227	If you have more than one social account, have you thought about cross promoting your content? For example, if you have written a LinkedIn article, then definitely use the link and promote that content on Twitter.	Mechanics
228	Are you clear about the problem you are trying to solve in your research? Spend 10 minutes writing a couple of sentences in plain language about this and reflect on this in future social posts.	Your research
229	Develop a post on your hidden talent.	Personal
230	Celebrate the work of a colleague who inspires you.	Inspire
231	We all have a to-do list, but what about your ta-dah list? Share the big and small things you've ticked off this week.	Academic life
232	Share a short-cut. What is something you do that makes life so much easier for your work?	Engagement/Advice
233	Who are the people behind the scenes at your work you could thank and show appreciation for?	Gratitude
234	Share a photo of when you did your PhD and explain what you needed to work through in order to finish. How has that informed your work now?	Your research

(Continued)

Table 4.2 (Continued)

Idea	Prompt	Theme
235	Remember the person you supported when they first started using social media? Go to their account and engage with their content. Send them a private message to encourage them.	Supportive
236	Create a "feel-good" playlist and share it.	Fun
237	Do 10 minutes of research today and find out what significant international days are coming up. What content can you plan for to support these? **Go a little deeper:** If there are any that align with you or your research area, can you do more substantial content?	Mechanics
238	Share a tidbit of a work in progress. How are you feeling about it?	Your research
239	Share a holiday post photo. Show your audience the fun part of your life.	Personal
240	Do you think architecture supports learning, teaching, and thinking? Take a snap of your favorite architectural features and share your experience.	Inspire
241	Post a picture of yourself at work.	Academic life
242	Share two of your favorite tips that you have learnt over time that could help people become better academic writers. **Go a little deeper:** Share a sample of your early work. What would you do differently? Does anything make you cringe?	Engagement/Advice
243	Did you know that some trees in Melbourne have email addresses? It was originally set up for people to report problems to council; instead, they send the trees love letters. Post a few thoughts about your favorite tree and what it adds to your life. Share a picture.	Gratitude
244	When you are preparing a paper, is there a time when you really hate it and think that it is worthless? How do you persevere and get it done?	Your research
245	Offer a brief tutorial of something you learnt or something related to your expertise.	Supportive
246	Create a post on other things that can be done instead of scrolling on social media	Fun
247	Reduce some of your mental load today. Find 10 inspiring quotes. Post one a week for the next 10 weeks. Pro tip: Use Canva to create a design for the quotes to add something beautiful to your posts.	Mechanics
248	Describe your research in only a few sentences and ask others to do the same.	Your research
249	Share a post on what you have learned this year so far.	Personal
250	Post one of the quotes you worked on three days ago. Revel in the ease of it. Then schedule the next nine in Tweet deck.	Inspire
251	Review the past week and cut down your biggest time waster.	Academic life
252	Tag someone you look up to and ask them for their #1 priority tip.	Engagement/Advice

(Continued)

Table 4.2 (Continued)

Idea	Prompt	Theme
253	We know life as an academic is challenging, especially in terms of workload, but in thinking about your career, what are you grateful for?	Gratitude
254	For research that is coming out in the next 12 months, who are the key audiences you'd like to reach? How can you use social media to do that? **Go a little deeper:** Start to follow new people in that sector. Your future self will thank you.	Your research
255	Share something you have accomplished this week that you thought may not have been possible. Was it something you finished? Was it some good news you have received? If you feel stuck for ideas, use this as an opportunity to celebrate a fellow colleague.	Supportive
256	Describe a favorite movie/book that makes you smile.	Fun
257	Spend some time using the 'for you' or 'explore' offerings on your social media platform. It's a good way to find new accounts to follow or discover trending content.	Mechanics
258	Remember your challenge from four days prior? Can you gather content now that will help with dissemination? Photos of the research in action, perhaps? Make a list of opportunities.	Your research
259	Share a travel bucket list. Tell your audience about the places you want to visit in the future.	Personal
260	Enjoy the glory of posts that you've already scheduled. It's OK to feel smug. We all do at times like this.	Inspire
261	Share "a day in my life" post. Post about different aspects of your day and how you spent your day productively.	Academic life
262	Share a short video of tips on a topic of your choice. It might be related to your usual work, for example, how to get research done efficiently or how to negotiate authorship order. It might be related to science communication, for example, an explainer on altmetrics or something about your work or research. Happy recording!	Engagement/Advice
263	Post a throwback about an achievement or an event you attended some time ago. Thank the people involved, as you are still feeling the flow-on effects. Include a photo.	Gratitude
264	For your latest research paper, try out a video editing tool like Adobe Sprout or Lumen 5 and make an under-60-seconds video with short text outlining your key findings. Post it with a link to the paper.	Your research
265	Share a challenge that you have had to overcome this week, how you managed to overcome it, and whether other people helped facilitate that. You don't need to mention names. In fact, you might just do a general shoutout to your colleagues in academia because the people we work with often provide an important source of social support.	Supportive
266	Have you tried to have new headshots taken? Share the bloopers.	Fun

(Continued)

Table 4.2 (Continued)

Idea	Prompt	Theme
267	Create your own hashtag that is significant to your work (e.g., your class or research topic). Encourage your audience to also use it so you can browse their content and choose the best to re-share with your audience. **Go a bit extra:** If you have a class, encourage students to engage in a class hashtag. Have them follow notable people concerned with the class topic or course and have them create posts that talk about who they followed and why or what they learned. Make sure they use the hashtag. Some educators assign credit points for such an activity.	Mechanics
268	Do you have an elevator pitch which describes your research? It's time to write or refine it.	Your research
269	Post your favorite picture and share the story behind it.	Personal
270	Share something that inspires you.	Inspire
271	Share your worries or concerns about your job (the research process, teaching, public speaking) and then how you overcome them. This is a sort of 'progress post'! People like to hear about your worries and concerns, especially if they are relatable. Go a little deeper: If you have managed to overcome them, then share exactly how you did it so that others will benefit from your advice.	Academic life
272	Share new learnings (or understandings) derived from recent research you have conducted (or even something new you have just read). It may be related to your design or method, not necessarily research findings. Don't forget to add the link!	Engagement/Advice
273	Has somebody been kind to you lately? Share how you felt and how it impacted your day.	Gratitude
274	Talk about pursuing your ambition in life. Is ambition a difficult word to talk about publicly?	Your research
275	Are any of your students graduating? Have they got a job? Send congratulations to them.	Supportive
276	What is the most ridiculous thing you've ever cried over? A television ad? Every time you hear a specific song? Share that, and ask your audience to share their experiences.	Fun
277	If you are posting on LinkedIn, remember to tag your colleagues who may have collaborated with you or are in a collective photo.	Mechanics
278	When sharing content about your research, ask yourself: What do you want your audience to do with this information?	Your research
279	Share the list of your hobbies. Ask others what you should try next.	Personal
280	Post a motivational quote of the day. This will motivate your audience to start the day refreshed.	Inspire
281	Feature one of your favorite co-workers. Talk about their support in accomplishing your tasks.	Academic life

(*Continued*)

Table 4.2 (Continued)

Idea	Prompt	Theme
282	Share an idea that didn't work for you. Talk about your perspective and reasons for failure. It can also be the trial and errors that you share with your followers.	Engagement/Advice
283	Do you have a view from your office window? Share what you like best about it.	Gratitude
284	Share something ironic in academia or your core research interest.	Your research
285	Did you recently attend a conference? Write a short LinkedIn article or compose a Tweet thread about your key takeaways. Remember to use the conference #hashtag and to tag any of the people you reference.	Supportive
286	Share something that you recently indulged in.	Fun
287	Do you follow your favorite social media platforms on their own channels? They are often full of tips and notifications of new features. Take a couple of minutes now to check out their feed and follow them.	Mechanics
288	For your next grant submission, can you include a budget line for research dissemination and impact? This might include things like producing an impact case study, commissioning photographs of your research in action, or hosting a participatory exhibition. All of this is valuable and shareable content that needs to be planned for.	Your research
289	Share what you are listening to. It can be a song or a podcast.	Personal
290	Share a picture of your weekly/monthly planner. Talk about the effectiveness of planning a week at the start, including a rough idea of what to post on social media.	Inspire
291	Talk about a current or past experience when revising one of your manuscripts after peer review.	Academic life
292	Share your tips and tricks for writing, editing, or proofreading. Create a 'how to guide' or short infographic containing one or two things you find helpful.	Engagement/Advice
293	Celebrate small wins. Share GIFs that best describe them.	Gratitude
294	Share a point of view on what you are currently working on.	Your research
295	Tag someone you admire most (it could be a family member, friend, relative, or anyone) and tell your audience why you admire that person.	Supportive
296	Post a meme that resonates with your research.	Fun
297	Are you ready to live tweet an event? Plan to do it for your next conference. Do your research in advance and gather the Twitter handles of the speakers. Follow them. **Pro tip:** Get some free visuals ready from a site like Unsplash.	Mechanics
298	Share a photo of what you have been struggling with at the moment.	Your research

(*Continued*)

Table 4.2 (Continued)

Idea	Prompt	Theme
299	Share a brief story about what you did in the past. It might mean talking about a time or experience as a graduate student or your experience in a past profession and how it might link to what you know about your current role. Bonus points if you can link it with your current research interest.	Personal
300	Share the account of someone you follow regularly for inspiration.	Inspire
301	Give your audience a glimpse into the inner workings of your work that aren't usually shared publicly. People like to see work behind-the-scenes, and it can be fun to get creative in your approach. For example, one colleague once posted a picture of a tree on his walk with the caption "this is how I start the writing process." It was a candid reminder that good work often takes careful thinking and time well before a letter is written on a page.	Academic life
302	Share hacks for every researcher that makes things easier.	Engagement/Advice
303	Share a short video of something you loved (it could be a place you visited, a food you tried for the first time, a new book purchased, etc.).	Gratitude
304	If you could make one thing that would put your research into the hands of people who could use it, what would it be? Can you put this into your future work plans?	Your research
305	Students often find it difficult to make friends, especially within those first few weeks in a new location with an entirely new group of people. Share your experiences and offer advice on what you did to negotiate the challenge or problem when you were in the same situation (when you started university perhaps). Suggest things to do with acquaintances or even list some conversation starters.	Supportive
306	Share a new experience you had. It can be related to your work, exploring a new restaurant, or a shopping place.	Fun
307	Share a link to a post that you've made on another social media platform. For example, some academics only occasionally use Twitter and prefer Instagram, so if they see someone they follow on Twitter is on Instagram, they're likely to follow you on Instagram.	Mechanics
308	What's in the news about your research area? Is there a comment that you can make that adds to the conversation?	Your research
309	Talk about your favorite childhood memory and share a picture.	Personal
310	Which academic inspires you on social media? What do you like about them? Are there any ways you can incorporate their approach into your socials?	Inspire

(Continued)

Table 4.2 (Continued)

Idea	Prompt	Theme
311	Share a recent negative or positive experience from your work being peer-reviewed.	Academic life
312	Share a tip that may be of value to your audience.	Engagement/Advice
313	Who are the professional staff in your faculty or school that support researchers? Give them a big shoutout today.	Gratitude
314	Use your social media platform to host a chat or Q&A on your preferred app. Alert your audience that it will be happening and encourage colleagues to promote it. You could invite your favorite person you interact with on social media as a guest for an informal interview.	Your research
315	Find and follow 10 early career researchers in your field and comment on their content.	Supportive
316	You'll never really know what your audience thinks, feels, or wants unless you ask them. Use a poll or ask a question to elicit their ideas on a topic. Or try something fun. Go a bit extra: To increase engagement, make it fun for your audience to answer – have them respond with a GIF!	Fun
317	If you have more than one social account, have you thought about cross-promoting your content? For example, if you have written a LinkedIn article, then definitely use the link and promote that content on Twitter.	Mechanics
318	Do you end up with documents with multiple comments? Share a screenshot to show what collaboration looks like. **Go a little deeper:** Do a screen recording of the collective process.	Your research
319	Share a list of your favorite podcasts.	Personal
320	How does nature support your capacity as a researcher? Share your favorite spot outdoors.	Inspire
321	Reveal just one aspect of how you engage in the research or writing process – start, finish, or somewhere in between. Or if you don't do research or write, perhaps you can share a lesson or session plan for teaching or even just an activity you do with staff or students.	Academic life
322	Share three things to do to ensure a productive week.	Engagement/Advice
323	Write a thank you post for your audience and express appreciation for their support.	Gratitude
324	Take a screenshot of you hitting 'submit' on a big paper. Celebrate the moment.	Your research
325	Share a paper you recently read and a screenshot of the abstract. Why was it interesting?	Supportive
326	Make and post a meme relevant to your field and highly relatable to your followers.	Fun

(*Continued*)

Table 4.2 (Continued)

Idea	Prompt	Theme
327	Do you have enough visual content? Sit down for five minutes today and plan out any upcoming opportunities to get images. Especially important are photos of you as a researcher in action, so you may need to swallow discomfort and ask for some support. **Go a little deeper**: Is there a way to organize professional photos that can capture your research in action?	Mechanics
328	Post a photo of a progress teaser of your recent work. This will help your audience figure out where the project is leading.	Your research
329	Share behind-the-scenes images of you at work.	Personal
330	Create a poll and ask people what they would like to see more of from you.	Inspire
331	Share your favorite resources that help your research (apps, website, blogs).	Academic life
332	Ask for advice on a task you are currently working on. This helps normalize the process of asking questions and not having all the answers.	Engagement/Advice
333	Share a song or quote that lifts you up and that makes you smile. **Go a little deeper:** Link it to your work or research interests. Tag and thank the person who made it.	Gratitude
334	SCITLDR is a tool that can summarize a paper abstract into a sentence. Try it with one of your older papers.	Your research
335	Share some of your favorite journals to read, review for, or publish in. Describe why.	Supportive
336	Share the list of weekend movies you recommend others to watch.	Fun
337	Time to sit down with an old-fashioned pen and paper and think about your goals on social media for the next three months. What pieces of content are valuable to your audience? Can you build in some time to create them? Pro tip: Articles that translate your research into plain English help put your research into the hands of people who can use it. Can you schedule some time to write them?	Mechanics
338	Create a short 'did you know?' video on anything you are specialized in to help those new to the field. You might discuss how something is defined or present an interesting fact.	Your research
339	Share a memory from your student life, travel diaries, or an event.	Personal
340	Who or what supports you in being creative in your thinking?	Inspire

(*Continued*)

Table 4.2 (Continued)

Idea	Prompt	Theme
341	What is something you hope to accomplish in the future? Share a dream. **Note:** For some, this post might feel a bit awkward, but if it does, you can always use the success or an achievement of someone else to leverage your ambition. You might share a post by somebody else who has accomplished something you admire. It might be something recent or old, and you could springboard their post and talk about how it is something you also want to achieve in the future. A post like this, particularly for early career researchers, can lead to opportunities. You'll never know who is watching.	Academic life
342	Post a list of the tools you use to write manuscripts.	Engagement/Advice
343	Has there been a time when criticism has strengthened your work? Thank your past self for having the resilience to listen to it.	Gratitude
344	Ask for help from someone who can assist you with a recent project or research.	Your research
345	Has a colleague written a piece lately on *the Conversation*? Make a supportive comment under the article.	Supportive
346	Tell me your favorite book without telling me the book. (It could be a phrase or a short quote from the book.)	Fun
347	Take a break from social media today. Have a cup of tea. Put your phone down. You've earned it.	Mechanics
348	Write an 800-word LinkedIn article with four subheadings which summarizes your latest research. Post with appropriate hashtags and tag your co-authors. **Go a bit extra:** Find great images to accompany it	Your research
349	Share a weekend getaway post with your friends and family.	Personal
350	Transformation Tuesday. It might not actually be Tuesday, but here's your chance to create a post describing a transformation. Perhaps it was a student who transformed their grade or your own personal accomplishment. People love to see photos if you can share. Try to keep this work-related.	Inspire
351	Identify your top five tasks last week that produced 80 percent of your result.	Academic life
352	Share a post on what a researcher or student can do if feeling tired, burnout, overwhelmed, or stressed while studying.	Engagement/Advice
353	Take a photo and share a place where you feel a sense of belonging in your workplace. Is it in the office, staff room, or classroom? Accompany this picture with a sentence about what makes you belong to your institution.	Gratitude

(*Continued*)

Table 4.2 (Continued)

Idea	Prompt	Theme
354	Extract a 15-30 second snippet from your audio presentation and create an audiogram video. An audiogram uses a static image (typically a picture of the presenter), a dynamic visualization of sound waves, and subtitles. There are various platforms for creating audiograms, but we recommend Headliner as they offer a generous free account for academics, and it has a user-friendly interface. These are useful for those who are hearing impaired but also for those who don't use sound when using social media.	Your research
355	What is something interesting you've learned from being a PhD supervisor? Go a bit extra: If appropriate, tag the student who taught you this lesson.	Supportive
356	Drop an emoji or GIF in response to content that you really enjoyed and found thought-provoking.	Fun
357	It's time for a yearly review of how you use social media to support your career values and goals. What has worked this year? What hasn't? What do you need to do more of? What can you stop doing? What will this look like for you in the next year?	Mechanics
358	Talk about what motivates you to work.	Your research
359	Take a picture of any books that you're reading at the moment. As a bonus, try and find the author on Twitter and tag them. You'll make their day!	Personal
360	Share the most interesting thing you've studied so far. This is the perfect opportunity to share your research passions.	Inspire
361	Open up about something on your mind. (It could be about your recent research, study, etc.)	Academic life
362	Share a list of active recall methods that can be used for remembering concepts.	Engagement/Advice
363	What have you learned from *An Academic's Guide to Social Media*? What surprised you the most? Share that and tag @socialacademics.	Gratitude
364	Write down one to three fears about social media and how you overcame them. Normalize the things that can feel uncomfortable on social media. We hope *An Academic's Guide to Social Media* helped you overcome your fears or awkwardness. **Go a bit further** and give *An Academic's Guide to Social Media* a plug!	Personal
365	Share a fact or tip from *An Academic's Guide to Social Media* and don't forget to tag us @drkellyallen @DrJ_ucsb @dsquintana @Lara_McKinley_ @SocialAcademics and use the hashtag #SocialAcademics.	Fun

The authors of this book hope that you will never be stumped on what to post on social media again. Tag us in your posts as we would love to see your work in progress!

@drkellyallen @DrJ_ucsb @dsquintana @Lara_McKinley_ @SocialAcademics

Video content

Social media platforms have a strong preference for video content and give video content preferential treatment in their algorithms. There are a huge range of formats available: think about TikTok, Instagram Reels, Stories (that disappear after 24 hours) or Facebook Lives. Academics have found videos to be another way to share expertise.

There is a lot of variety as well in the kinds of videos that are posted. For academics, this content can be explainer videos, story-based case-study videos, moderated seminars and relatable updates via stories. And that's just the start.

According to Sprout Social (Coleman, 2022), people share video content twice as much as other content. Tweets with video get 2.5x the replies, 2.8x more retweets, 1.9x more likes, and 10x more engagement. On Instagram, 91% of users watch videos weekly, nearly half prefer Instagram stories. Facebook users report they are 4x more likely to watch Facebook Live videos. More than 100 billion hours of video are consumed daily.

Videos take longer to produce than simple text or image-based content, but you are rewarded not only with better reach and engagement but also better understanding from your audience. People have been shown to have far better recall of information from watching a video over reading a text (Vanichvasin, 2021; Yadav et al., 2011). While research in this area is still developing, it's worth at least pondering your own feelings about video vs. text content. Does storytelling through video feel more engaging to you compared to text? Would you feel brave enough to star in one of the videos?

Here are five different ways you can incorporate video into your social platforms.

1. **Stories**

    Stories are short videos that disappear after 24 hours. Capture them on your smartphone for a reasonably low risk way to get started on video and create authentic, behind-the-scenes content.

    Most social platforms offer them, and you can typically see a story has been posted by the person's profile picture being encircled by a color bubble. They are increasingly popular among users, particularly on Instagram, although they didn't perform well on Twitter (these were known as "fleets") and were phased out.

    Using video on Stories is just one way to use the function on socials – you can create polls, link to external content, and use them to share your recent posts.

If you are doing a video story you will need to shoot vertically, make sure you have good quality audio and clean your phone's cameras. If your clip is under 60 seconds, then Instagram will cut it up for you. Try not to over-think it.

2. **TikTok and Reels**

   TikTok and Instagram's (Reels) feature short form video content can either be created in-platform – and come with all kinds of tools to make the process easy and fun – or uploaded from your phone. TikToks were initially limited to 15 seconds but can now be up to three minutes and are being trialed at 10 minutes. Reels can be up to 60 seconds. Snapchat and Pinterest have also launched a TikTok-like feature.

   These videos are designed to be fun, snackable pieces of content. Unlike other platforms, there is no expectation of high production values, as most videos are captured using a smartphone. There are often viral challenges users can jump on board with, and a strong sense of community can develop around these. The best way to learn to do these videos is by doing it. So, if this is something that your audience will respond to, jump on board, and give it a go.

3. **Story-based videos**

   Most social media platforms allow you to upload video content that you have created to share on your feed. The maximum length of these varies from platform to platform – as does the ideal length (which are often two different things). Video formats also differ from platform to platform.

   It is thought that humans have evolved to respond to stories, as this helps boost cooperation, something that was crucial for the survival of our ancestors (Smith et al., 2017). It's why story-based content works. It's why big brands focus on story-based ads during the Superbowl, and it's why non-profit organizations focus on people-based stories in fundraising.

   This is where the opportunity lies for academics. An audit of the top universities shows there is very little video content that tells the story of research impact through the eyes of the people and communities it benefits. But when you can capture that story, it not only shows the impact of your research but can also increase it.

   Story-based content takes time, money, and effort to create. Unless you are very technically minded, you will likely need a professional team to produce the story. It's worth planning and budgeting for at the start of the project because not only can you use it on your own social media channels, but your institutional social account managers – along with your donors and funders – will likely love it.

   When working with a professional team, you will need to be very clear that you want to use interviews and visual overlays to create a story-based video. Spend time in your planning phase to really go over what the film will look like, what it will sound like, and then write a very good brief.

   One final thing to bear in mind for story-based videos. It's important to remember who the hero of your piece is and to focus on them. Scripted content rarely works for people who are not actors, so it's best to avoid. If you make it too much of an exercise in profiling your institution, and make your institution the hero, your video will have a 'corporate stink' to it, and audiences – who are very savvy at picking up advertising – will switch off.

4. **Lives**

If you are on a social media platform, you pretty much have access to your own broadcasting platform. Most social platforms have the capacity to livestream content from your smartphone in a few quick clicks.

Lives are often pushed out as preferential content by the platforms, so you will likely receive more eyeballs on your content, and you can interact with your audience in real time. It's a great way of sharing expertise, delivering a mini-lecture, or inviting another person in to host a live conversation.

Unless you are a natural performer, it pays to be very well prepared when hosting a live video. Have a series of 'beats' or topics you plan to cover. Have a contingency plan if there is no one on the live or people aren't interacting so you can keep delivering what you planned. Lives will be posted on your timeline once they are finished (although on Instagram you have to opt-in to save it before you go live).

It's worth not trying to do this alone – try to have a support person help you manage each live and any technical issues that may arise.

5. **Explainer videos**

Unlike story-based content, explainer videos are common ways for researchers to produce video content so that non-specialist audiences can understand it. Explainer videos allow you to break down complex ideas into bite-sized pieces and to harness the advantages of video content on your socials.

They often use a combination of short pieces of text and footage to pull together the explanation. It's a common and effective way news organizations – particularly print media – translate their stories for social media.

There are several video-editing apps you can use to do this. Some of our favorites are Adobe Spark or Adobe Premiere Rush, and the online platform Lumen 5. Try to keep your video under 60 seconds and the pieces of text short and sharp. For example, in a 60-second video you would aim for under 100–150 words.

Another kind of explainer video is a straightforward mini-lecture, explaining a concept. You can use them to launch a new piece of research, break down key points around your research theme, or use to expand the reach of your teaching. Eddie Woo – a Sydney-based maths teacher – does this very effectively on his YouTube channel, 'Woo Tube.'

Your institution will also have corporate branding guidelines, so follow these as closely as possible, and be sure to sense-check what you've produced with a colleague before publishing. (Figure 4.1).

Figure 4.1 Using video content on social media can be engaging for your audience and evidence for this comes from the rapid uptake and popularity of various video-based platforms such as TikTok.

Source: Photo by Amanda Vick on Unsplash

CASE STUDY: TikTok, accessible and easily accessed

By Paul Harrison, Department of Marketing, Deakin University, Burwood, Australia (@drpaulharrison on TikTok)

I've always thought that one of the key roles of an academic is to talk about our research. To talk about it to as many people as possible. And yet, for the most part, the academy tends to use a single source of media for the dissemination of its knowledge; the journal article. Which really only talks to other academics and research professionals.

But with the emergence of all of the different social media platforms, we now have an opportunity to talk to so many different audiences about our research.

I started my first blog in 2007 as a way to talk about my research interests to a broad audience. It initially had a small reach, but as I appeared more and more on mainstream media, I started to reach a wider audience. Between 2007 and 2020, I tried podcasts, a YouTube site, Twitter, tumblr, and Facebook, along with writing for online sources such as The Conversation, FinderX, and also writing and appearing in mainstream media as a means to get people outside of academia as excited about the research I was doing as I was.

But in 2020, I discovered (like a lot of us) that we weren't allowed to leave the house.

And with that, discovered TikTok. It took me a while to fully understand how the whole thing worked, but I realised that I didn't need to lip sync or do dances to pick up an audience. I made a short announcement – a video telling people that I did research in the area of human behaviour – and asked whether people were interested in it. I posted it on TikTok and forgot about it for a couple of hours. However, over a period of a week I went from two followers to nearly 30,000 followers. I now have around 75,000 followers who are interested in research around human behaviour. And although the pandemic is settling somewhat, the interest in my videos continues.

Depending on my mood and my workload, I like to do at least one video every few weeks. In the early days, to build up an audience, I was doing one or two videos per week. The thing is, the reason I do the videos is not because I'm provided with the workload or that I get paid, but because I really enjoy talking about this subject. There have been some bumps along the way, particularly in relation to questioning why I was doing what I was doing. But I'm a grown-up; I just needed to reassess what was important and make decisions about my motivations for being on the platform.

Over the years, I've learnt a whole bunch of skills related to talking about mine and other's research, from audio and video editing, how to compress a complex idea into 160 characters, and even how to get research opportunities simply because you have a social media presence.

For example, because of a TikTok video I was contacted by a government department and asked to advise on the rollout of a behaviour *change program. As a result of my appearance on free to air television program, I was contacted [as] an expert witness in a copyright case in the Federal court. Obviously these outcomes don't happen in a direct line, but what having a social media presence does is give you a profile that you wouldn't have if you weren't there. And as many of us know, in the absence of other information, you become an expert simply because you are visible.*

Clearly social media isn't for everyone. But it is such an accessible (to an outside audience) and easily accessed (to the content provider), that it is worth considering.

A word about gear and other technical stuff

There are a few technical things to keep in mind when producing video content. Always aim for the best possible audio. Avoid windy situations and, where you can, use a microphone or at the very least headphones with a built-in microphone.

Unless you are going for a jilted and bouncy effect, consider using a tripod, fitted with a smartphone mount. Although most modern smartphones come with incredible image-stabilizing software, the tripod, especially for lives, will help keep the picture clean and you free of distractions while talking. The back camera is a better-quality option than the front (selfie) one if you have a support person who can help. It's important to include subtitles on your video content (either as SRT caption files, auto-generated in-platform captions, or captions burned into the files) for both access for the hearing-impaired and for people who watch social media on silent.

One final piece of video wisdom – especially when producing story-based feed content: Always try to put your most compelling and interesting point at the very beginning of your video. Our attention spans are short, and you've got only a few moments to capture the eyeballs of the audience. If you don't hook them in these first few moments, they scroll past. You can see the drop-off in the video analytics on your platform.

Part III
Taking a deeper dive

5 Maintaining a social media presence

Academics don't need to constantly post on social media to stay relevant, but it does give us outsiders a wonderful insight into what you're working on, which is always interesting

@GoatsLive

Introduction

In Chapter 2, we looked at aligning your social media presence with your career and research, values, and goals. Take a moment now to revisit those, as they become the foundation of how you can sustainably maintain a social media presence. This chapter explores how your social media presence can be maintained without becoming a burden.

Finding the time

We have found the most common barrier with academics is time. It is important to acknowledge the considerable workload pressures facing most academics – between teaching, research, publishing, and supervision, there's not a lot of room in an academic schedule.

Many academics feel overworked, under pressure, and in a battle to meet work demands. Often this occurs while balancing home duties, a teaching load, and an ambition for achieving metrics that may one day result in career progression. However, if you can reframe your social media presence to serve these other areas of academic life, then it becomes something that amplifies the work that you are already doing. Take PhD supervision: social media interactions are a simple, and time effective, way to support your students, stay engaged with their community, amplify their work, and attract new candidates.

In terms of research, social media can support the recruitment process for your study. In 2018, Monash Education researcher Amanda Heffernan et al. (2022) conducted what was then Australia's biggest survey of teachers and educators – recruited through strong existing networks but also simple social media call-outs for people to take part. That call-out turned out to be one of the top performing pieces of content of the year for their faculty.

DOI: 10.4324/9781003198369-8

Think about publishing: having a good social media presence and a consistent way you promote your published papers will increase your citations (Finch et al., 2017; Quintana & Doan, 2016; Smith et al., 2019), awareness of your work, as well as putting your research into the hands of people who wouldn't necessarily search for it in a journal. The list goes on.

Social media, when aligned with your values, becomes a very effective use of your time to achieve your goals and amplify your work. Like other tasks in your day, it can be diarized and ticked off. We will cover some advice about the logistical aspects of this in the subsequent sections.

How fear plays a role in not having time

But if it was that simple, then maintaining a social media presence would be easy. But there is another aspect of "not having time" that is based less on time management and more on fear. That is when the issue of time becomes an excuse.

The fear then transforms maintaining a social media presence into something you feel guilty about, something you "should do" but don't. It feels heavy, onerous, and an overwhelming obligation. Fear manifests itself in several ways:

- Avoiding posting because you think you don't have anything interesting to say
- Spending too much time writing a simple tweet or post
- Imposter syndrome – others are doing this so much better than you
- Fear of looking stupid or doing it wrong
- Thinking you will destroy your career by making a mistake
- Being a *lurker*, rather than an active member of the community
- And most commonly, fear of *big noting* yourself, showing off

And this is just the beginning. No wonder it becomes something to avoid. There's a lot going on there.

- Gendered responses to positioning yourself as an expert
- Cultural responses to self-promotion
- Creative (and paralyzing) perfectionism
- Discomfort with being a beginner

This is where your values and goals can really kick in. They help you to develop a plan of action not only to manage the logistics of maintaining a social presence but also in tackling the fears that come with it. The process looks something like this: Values > Goals > Three-month plan with specific numbers > Weekly tactics (Figure 5.1).

Developing a plan of action

Let's take Nicola Chan (name has been deidentified), an early career researcher who wants to develop her career, build new research collaborations, and put her

Figure 5.1 Your goals and values are pivotal to implementing your plan of action on social media.

Source: Photo by Estée Janssens on Unsplash

research into the hands of people who will use it. She suspects social media can support her in this and is willing to commit a little time to test the waters.

Nicola has a neglected Twitter account she started at the beginning of her PhD. Her LinkedIn account is up to date, but she rarely posts and has never written an article. Facebook is a channel she uses for family and friends, and Instagram is for photos of her labradoodle. Working through the process, she has determined her values, goals, and strategy.

Her values:
1   Do research that has an impact.
2   Be part of supportive academic networks.
3   Challenge myself.

Her goals:
1   Disseminate the findings of my PhD.
2   Develop two new research collaborations.
3   Publish a new paper in an influential journal for my field.
4   Work towards promotion.
5   Build a professional network.

Her three-month strategy:
1   Identify key audiences.
    a   People who can use my research.
    b   Potential collaborators.

    c   Journal editors.

    d   Leadership in Faculty.

2   Build a social media presence.

    a   Identify and follow 60 specific people from those audiences on chosen channels.

    b   Create regular content that is interesting to those audiences.

    c   Engage with those audiences weekly.

    d   Identify, follow, and use five specific and strategic hashtags.

    e   Boost visibility of self and work (which will lead to increased citations, invitations to present, and recognition of leadership).

3.   Translate research findings and expertise for non-academic audiences.

    a   Use plain language articles.

    b   Employ infographics.

    c   Pitch *The Conversation* with a story idea.

By being strategic about whom she is following and engaging with on her social media, Nicola begins to curate her feed and that aligns her research interests. It also means that when she is ready to disseminate research findings, she's got an audience that will be receptive to it.

This can then be broken up into weekly tactics that cover those tasks, including content creation. Always coming up with something to post can be mentally draining, but it is also something you can plan for (check out our 365 content and engagement prompts in Chapter 4).

Types of content to consider

1   Research translation (articles and infographics)

2   Retweets or reposts that share opinions, expertise, or reflections

3   Updates on projects and activities, including photos

4   Lighter content (e.g., memes/dog/academic life reflections)

5   Advice/behind the scenes

Weekly tactics

After setting her goals, Nicola has determined that Twitter and LinkedIn are the channels she will focus on, with a loose commitment to be active on Twitter five days a week for 10 minutes a day and engage on LinkedIn once a week for 10 minutes. Once a month she is going to translate a piece of her work into plain language, either as a blog or LinkedIn article.

She's developed the weekly tactical plan (below) to reduce the burden of what to post as well as tackling the discomfort that she feels about "putting herself out there." Where there are key events that are coming up (e.g., a conference), Nicola can tweak her plan to incorporate this. Conferences are terrific ways to both be a good social media citizen and gather new followers.

Monday: Community Day: Connect and engage with a target audience (people who can use research), find new people to follow, actively engage with key people (like posts, comments, and thoughtful retweets)

Tuesday: Share key findings from PhD (either a blog post, an infographic designed in Canva, a tweet thread (series of tweets), or monthly LinkedIn article).

Wednesday: Support a colleague/researcher/collaborator/PhD student with a reflection. Engage with target academic journals.

Thursday: Share behind-the-scenes content about what I'm working on. Be brave and include a photo every two weeks. When not feeling brave, post a photo of dog, organizational systems, or workspace.

Friday: Community Day: Connect and engage a target audience (academic leaders), find new people to follow, actively engage with key people (like posts, comments, and thoughtful retweets)

When developing your weekly tactical plan, please feel free to use the #SocialAcademics prompts from Chapter 4.

Importance of consistency and timing

Social media has a definite momentum and flow to it. For it to be an effective tool, it does require time and attention and that can be a big commitment from people who are already stretched. It's about being smart with the time you can commit to it, and it's about recognizing the "social" part of "social media."

Social platforms prefer people to create "sticky" content – this means content that gets engagement and holds people on their page. For example, on Twitter this means that tweets with lots of replies, retweets, and likes are considered tweets with high engagement. So it is important not just to create content but engage and respond. If you take a break, it does take more time to get that engagement fired up and working for you again.

An analysis of data from the Twitter community at Monash University that has been running for the past three years has revealed – not surprisingly – a strong correlation between the number of tweets and follower growth. So for Nicola, her weekly tactical plan will help her remain consistent.

There are many social media scheduling platforms that can allow you to batch up your content into a single, focused session. The advantage is that you can post at peak times for your audience. Increasingly, these come at a cost, but there are some still available for free. For example, Hootsuite offers a very limited free plan that allows you to schedule two accounts and five posts. TweetDeck (now owned by Twitter and available for free for all Twitter users), allows you to schedule your tweets, follow hashtags, and manage multiple accounts. With all social media, it's important not to set and forget and to still engage with your audiences.

Plain language articles

These can be an effective way to put research into the hands of people who can use it. By writing simply and in plain language you can meet the audience where they are at: usually busy and without access to academic journals. Plain language articles (blogs, *The Conversation*, opinion pieces, and articles that can be written on personal LinkedIn accounts) are also excellent content to share on social media. Newsletter services, like Substack, are also growing in popularity to share longform writing.

It is a very smart move to write them on the back of a published academic paper or keynote presentation. You've already done the work, and this strategy takes advantage of that. There are a few simple tips when writing:

- Put the most important idea at the beginning and make it relevant to your audience.
- Write clear headlines and subheadings so people can scan and read the piece. This also helps people find you on Google.
- Stick to one idea per sentence and be clear in what you are trying to say.
- Use active voice and try to take out qualified language.
- Aim for an 800–1000-word count for articles, 400–500 words for opinion pieces.

Be informed by your data

Social media comes with some powerful tools to see what is working and what isn't working when it comes to your posts. Social platforms have algorithms that determine how many people will see your content. Algorithms change all the time but, put simply, the more people who have engaged with your content – and the more active you are in responding – relates to the number of people who will see your content. Another reason not to "post and ghost."

There are key metrics you can follow over time:

- Follower growth Impressions or reach: This means how many accounts your content has reached
- Engagement: This means how many people have interacted with your content (like, share, comment)
- Link clicks: how many people click on links you are sharing

By checking in once a month you can adapt your tactics and plans. See for yourself the difference a photograph or video can make to a post's reach. Watch to see the impact of personal content as well. Try to focus on what is working (and do more of that) rather than what didn't work.

Hashtags are your friend

Hashtags are a good way to push out your content to a wider audience than the people who are following you, especially on platforms like Twitter, Instagram, and LinkedIn. Try to be strategic with your use of them. Find the top two or three hashtags used by your audiences – for example #academictwitter – and use those consistently.

Figure 5.2 Hashtags are important for finding your true audience #SocialAcademics.

Source: Photo by Jan Baborák on Unsplash

If you have a research project, think about what your consistent and unique #hashtag will be for that, even if you don't have a social presence for that particular project. You can then do a search and see how many mentions you get for it.

You can also use trending hashtags like #MotivationMonday, #TipTuesday, #WisdomWednesday, #ThankfulThursday, #FollowFriday, #SelfieSaturday, and #SelfcareSunday to create different days of the week. Other popular hashtags can be things like #TopicTuesday, #WellnessWednesday, #ThinkPositiveThursday, #FridayNight, #SpotlightSunday, or #SundayFunday – these can be helpful in generating ideas.

Don't forget you can also use made up hashtags to inject humor into your content as well. Think about what kind of post might go with something like #sorrynotsorry or #thedogdidactuallyeatmyhomework (Figure 5.2).

Celebrate whenever you can

Celebrate popular holidays, special days, occasions, and international days (Christmas, Hanukkah, New Year, Chinese New year, Ramadan and Eid al-Fitr, Easter, Valentine's day, Diwali, Halloween, Bodhi day, etc.) Use opportunities to celebrate other people's successes or interesting news to build a community.

Find the joy

We all love working with social media because it interrupts traditional, sometimes hierarchical, academic structures. Connections happen more easily, opportunities and collaborations can be fostered across the world, and we can be far more instrumental in the dissemination of our research beyond academic journals. It's good to inject humor – even if it's self-deprecating humor – to bring a smile to other people's day.

Figure 5.3 Social media can play an important role in your research and online identity, be kind.

Source: Photo by Braydon Anderson on Unsplash

Social media can be fun, a place where we can feel a part of a community, where we can support each other and celebrate our successes. Like anything new, there is a period when you feel deeply uncomfortable, as you are learning the language, the etiquette, and what works for you. And the biggest way of avoiding many of the pitfalls of social media? Be kind: to yourself and to others (Figure 5.3).

CASE STUDY: My motivation for social media

By Nicole Rinehart, Krongold Clinic Director of Research and Professor of Child and Adolescent Psychology, Monash University

What made me get into social media? It's absolutely imperative. We all want our research to be communicated. We all want it to be heard and to be useful. That's why we do research. But we were just never trained to do social media. Everything else we do as academics we are trained in, and we know exactly what to do.

It's taken me a while to get the hang of social media because you feel anxious as an academic about putting yourself out there like that. We just don't do that. We are not trained like that. It's a completely different language. It's a personal language, it's about your passion. Even what you like and respond to is telling the world something about you.

We're trained to be so incredibly conservative and careful, but everything has shifted quickly to impact for research. I think that's where the anxiety comes in. It feels like a big pressure as well, Like oh my God, I'm going to make a mistake. I'm not processing the rules as fast as I would like!

I decided to focus on LinkedIn and Twitter. I'm most comfortable on LinkedIn. I didn't really understand how to use it at first. I had just set it up, posted one or two things, and accepted connections.

I didn't understand how it could help start conversations and get impact for research. The first article I wrote there was after I started a new job. When you make a transition as a researcher, there's a lot of noise and you need a really clean, quick voice out to the community and that's what the LinkedIn article enabled.

It was really important in terms of re-establishing my profile, who I am and where I'm going. To be able to show optimism, and to connect with people. It was really personal.

I'm starting to get the knack of seeing synergies in what I'm doing, seeing how it's adding value and giving more return on investment for time. There was a virtual online conference for principals I spent ages preparing for. And it was a really great audience. Instead of throwing the talk in the bin, I wrote a LinkedIn article and it became a public record.

It enabled people who weren't at the meeting to engage in it. It enabled people who were at the meeting to share it. So in terms of return on investment, that's where you get bang for your buck. It's very satisfying.

It's been really lovely to get to know a different side of people and connect to a wide variety, not just academics but industry and government, and watch what they are doing.

Then that's really informing impactful research and how we're developing ideas.

I've had many stops and starts at it. Cutting words out, being clearer in communication has a fantastic effect on my scientific writing. I'm better at it now than I was. I am fortunate to be in a Faculty that invests in social media support for academics. Our Faculty leadership has built a positive and productive culture around social media to give lift and impact to our research.

In the future I think social media is going to play a big part in my research, but it's really dependent on me getting into that flow. Of all the advice that's been given to me, the most important is to have it as a regular tool that connects every activity and getting the whole research group involved. It becomes a part of the team culture.

A final thought about maintaining your engagement

Being an active and engaged user on social media and developing engaging content is only part of the story. As you will see in Chapters 7, social media use can expose academics to risks that are sometimes hard to avoid. Being prepared and informed will allow social media users to be equipped when trolls or bullies emerge as they inevitably do.

6 Controlling the trolls and other online misadventures

> PSA: Remember that trolls live under the bridges we create. They grunt and grumble and thrive in dank, dark spaces, but their presence is inconsequential. Keep building those bridges. Your work matters.
>
> @KeianaMayfield

Introduction

While freedom of speech and expression of diverse perspectives, ideas, information, and opinions are important to many people, it is also vital that social media facilitate safe and civil communication. Some groups of people are more likely than others to be targeted with abuse, bullying, or victimization online. Those most likely to be targeted include women, people of color, LGTBQ+ individuals, and others who are part of marginalized and historically underrepresented communities. Those among us who identify with multiple minoritized or marginalized groups are more likely to be the targets of toxic and harmful online discourse. Thus, it is imperative that social media users and platforms are aware and committed to preventing and addressing abuse motivated by hatred, prejudice, or intolerance.

Unfortunately, hateful conduct is pervasive across social media platforms. Using contemporary detection tools, many social media platforms (e.g., Facebook, YouTube, Instagram, Twitter) have increasingly reported flagging or removing content. For instance, during the first three months of 2021, Facebook removed more than 25 million pieces of content and Instagram removed more than 6 million. YouTube removed more than 85,000 videos that violated their hate speech policy. In Twitter's 2021 transparency report, the company removed more than 1.6 million pieces of content identified as violating their hate speech policy between July and December 2020. Contemporary detection tools are invaluable in helping to identify and remove such items, but there are many others that users may find offensive that may not be detected by these automated tools. Facebook was the only platform that reported prevalence metrics as of 2021, reporting that during the first three months of 2021, there was a small prevalence of hate speech (0.05%–0.06%), which was a decrease relative to previous reporting periods.

DOI: 10.4324/9781003198369-9

Identifying and addressing inappropriate and hateful online conduct

Online trolling, rage, hate, and victimization are examples of inappropriate, unacceptable, and abhorrent antisocial behaviors. Unfortunately, toxic behaviors are pervasive in social media and online environments. Many social media systems aim to reduce such malevolent content by using filters that employ algorithms to identify and eliminate the most toxic posts. Furthermore, most social platforms include user guidelines that prohibit such communications. For instance, the Twitter Rules outline acceptable and unacceptable behaviors and contents "to ensure all people can participate in the public conversation freely and safely" (see https://help. twitter.com/en/rules-and-policies/twitter-rules).

Twitter also has a detailed Hateful Conduct Policy to guide and inform appropriate social media use. Regarding hateful conduct, Twitter delineates

> *You may not promote violence against or directly attack or threaten other people on the basis of race, ethnicity, national origin, caste, sexual orientation, gender, gender identity, religious affiliation, age, disability, or serious disease. We also do not allow accounts whose primary purpose is inciting harm towards others on the basis of these categories.*
> (see https://help.twitter.com/en/rules-and-policies/hateful-conduct-policy)

Twitter also has policies addressing Abusive Behavior:

> *You may not engage in the targeted harassment of someone, or incite other people to do so. We consider abusive behavior an attempt to harass, intimidate, or silence someone else's voice.*
> (see https://help.twitter.com/en/rules-and-policies/abusive-behavior)

Indeed, it is unfortunate that such policies and laws are necessary to regulate the behaviors of some individuals and groups. In the United States, most states have established legislation and laws to address harassment and cyberbullying via electronic means. For instance, New York State Bill S7275, or the "social media hate speech accountability act":

> *prohibits hate speech on internet platforms and social media networks; defines terms; provides that the provider of a social media network shall maintain an effective and transparent procedure for handling complaints about hate speech content; authorizes attorney general enforcement; further authorizes up to one million dollars for a violation; makes related provisions.*

Recognizing the imperative of regulating online safety, the Parliament of U.K. Online Safety Bill (see https://en.wikipedia.org/wiki/Online_Safety_Bill), in development since 2021, includes minimum standards against which a provider's actions, systems, and processes to tackle harm, including automated or algorithmic content moderation, should be judged. This Bill delineates a new duty of care that would apply to all online platforms.

Do we really need laws against cyber hate to recognize that engaging in such behavior is morally and ethically unacceptable? Contextualizing bad behavior into narrow categories could help support perpetrators who are shielded by a lack of leg-islation. It may also trivialize behavior by associating it with a particular context when the behavior breaches social norms in most situations. Rapidly developing technolo-gies almost guarantee a lag in appropriate legislation to protect members of society.

It is in our individual and collective best interests to demand a set of socially acceptable behaviors that apply to all online contexts. The social etiquette that we use in day-to-day life should translate to our behavior online.

For many who access news on social media sites such as Facebook, the replies and comments are as informative as reading the article itself. However the bullying and trolling are most likely to appear in these sections. Whereas, many may be offended momentarily by inappropriate content directed at another person, unfor-tunately, most social media users continue to scroll past and read other comments without responding or reporting each instance of inappropriate content.

The general experience of being bystanders to abuse, racism, and bullying may be a product of disinhibition; which is commonly used to encourage the bad behavior of others online. Trends in behaviors suggest that few of us identifying inappropriate online content are likely to report inappropriate content or to address perpetrators. In some instances, if we were to experience the same behavior in real life, behaving as a passive bystander may risk legal consequences. Given the social distancing and anonymity of social media, responding to inappropriate con-tent is relatively limited.

In general, we encourage socially appropriate behavior across all contexts, cir-cumstances, always, for all people. We advocate for each of us to raise the bar regarding our expectations from others and actively engage to report and call out all instances of abuse or inappropriate content. Victims and the vulnerable need the support of others because the delineation between online and offline worlds is quickly vanishing. The way we treat and act towards one another needs constant consideration as our behavior transcends time and place and can have a wide-reaching impact (Figure 6.1).

A brief description of online toxic behavior

For those engaging in social media, the following provides a brief overview of some toxic behaviors that you may experience when participating in social media. The word toxic may mean different things to different people. Technically speak-ing, toxic describes substances that can cause harm, such as poisonous chemicals. However, in the context of online communications, it's a term often used to define behavior that is unpleasant or malicious towards others. The phrase "toxic posts" may be used to describe content that is subtly or directly aimed at being demean-ing, pejorative, hurtful, or harmful towards another.

- Trolls on social media are people who deliberately start arguments in the comments sections of sites. Trolling is when someone comments or responds to a post usually in a confrontational way that is designed to garner a strong, emotional reaction.
- A hater is someone who voices negative opinions about other people.

Figure 6.1 It is assumed that all members of a social media community will act in a socially acceptable way, but this is not always the case.

Source: Photo by Markus Winkler on Unsplash

- *Griefing* is when a user focuses on disrupting and annoying another person on purpose. This can involve a range of behaviors that are deliberate and aimed at *giving someone grief.*
- Hateful and abusive speech can take many forms including racism, anti-semitism, anti-Islamism, misogyny, and anti-LGBTQ+ abuse, among others.

Additional potential toxic activities to be aware of include those described in user safety materials available from many social media platforms. Table 6.1 includes a summary of communications that are identified in the Twitter Hateful Conduct Policy.

Addressing toxic social media communications

What can you do to address toxic social media communications? Block, mute, report, save evidence, and move on can be effective strategies to address toxic social

Table 6.1 A summary of communications that are identified as inappropriate in the Twitter Hateful Conduct Policy

---

Violent threats are declarative statements of intent to inflict injuries that would result in serious and lasting bodily harm, where an individual could die or be significantly injured, e.g., "I will kill you."

Wishing, hoping or calling for serious harm on a person or group of people includes content that promotes, incites, or expresses a desire for death, serious bodily harm, or serious disease against an entire protected category and/or individuals who may be members of that category.

Incitement against protected categories includes targeting individuals and groups with the intent to incite fear or spread fearful stereotypes about a protected category; this may include asserting that members of a protected category are more likely to take part in dangerous or illegal activities, e.g., "all [religious group] are terrorists."

References to mass murder, violent events, or specific means of violence where protected groups have been the primary targets or victims includes targeting individuals or groups by referencing forms of violence with an intent is to harass.

Repeated and/or non-consensual slurs, epithets, racist and sexist tropes, or other content that degrades someone includes targeting others with repeated content that intends to dehumanize, degrade, or reinforce negative or harmful stereotypes about a protected category. This includes targeted misgendering or deadnaming of transgender individuals or the dehumanization of a group of people based on their religion, caste, age, disability, serious disease, national origin, race, ethnicity, gender, gender identity, or sexual orientation.

Hateful imagery includes logos, symbols, or images whose purpose is to promote hostility and malice against others based on their race, religion, disability, sexual orientation, gender identity or ethnicity/national origin.

Adapted from https://help.twitter.com/en/rules-and-policies/hateful-conduct-policy

media behaviors. Most social media platforms provide mechanisms to avoid further interactions and allow for reporting toxic behavior to be regulated by the platform.

The first step is to locate the function within the social media platform that allows you to block and/or mute the communications from the individual. Depending upon the platform, such actions may disallow the individual from sharing communications with you. In addition, most platforms have a function to report the unsettling communications. In some instances, such reports may result in the perpetrator receiving sanctions for violating the rules on the platform. An example of enforcement policies is provided by Twitter with enforcement that may focus either on a specific piece of content (e.g., an individual tweet or direct message), or on an account, or both (https://help.twitter.com/en/rules-and-policies/enforcement-philosophy). Also, take screenshots to save evidence so you have documentation; if hate speech is continual, you may also have grounds for legal action. Although all hate speech is not necessarily illegal due to freedom of speech laws, it can be a criminal offense under harassment or cyberbullying laws. The other advice is to *move on*; it is generally most adaptive to avoid engaging with such posts, as it is unlikely that discussion, explanation, or exploration with an individual with malicious intent will be beneficial in the online social media context.

Importantly, there are numerous online resources addressing online bullying and trolling that you may consider. See for instance those listed in Table 6.2.

Table 6.2 Online resources addressing online bullying and trolling

- Anti-Bullying Alliance
  The Anti-Bullying Alliance is a coalition of organizations and individuals that are united against bullying. In addition to the United Against Bullying program, UAB also orchestrates a number of programs that focus on specific aspects of bullying behavior.
- Anti-Bullying Institute
  The Anti-Bullying Institute (ABI) was established to offer hands-on programs, services, and resources designed to empower children, parents, schools, and youth organization personnel to effectively deal with the issue of bullying. ABI advocates student and parent-centered bullying prevention education, and also HERO alumni through their ongoing programs.
- Born This Way Foundation
  The Born This Way Foundation (BTWF) builds youth-focused programs and engaging campaigns that increase access to resources, drive action, and build community. BTWF works to promote the mental health and wellness of youth by making kindness cool, validating the emotions of young people, and eliminating the stigma around mental health.
- It Gets Better Project
  The It Gets Better Project's mission is to uplift, empower, and connect lesbian, gay, bisexual, transgender, and queer (LGBTQ+) youth around the globe. The It Gets Better Project is a global non-profit that reaches millions of young people each year through inspiring media programming, educational resources, and international affiliates in 19 countries.
- Megan Meier Foundation
  The Megan Meier Foundation (MMF) was founded by Tina Meier in 2007 after her daughter Megan took her own life following a cruel cyberbullying hoax by an adult neighbor posing as a fictitious boy on MySpace. MMF has grown into a global bullying and cyberbullying prevention foundation providing education, prevention, and intervention to support and inspire actions to end bullying, cyberbullying, and suicide.
- Stand for the Silent
  Stand for the Silent is an anti-bullying organization, focused on bringing awareness to bullying and the real devastation it causes. Stand for the Silent was started in 2010 by a group of high school students in Oklahoma City, OK, after they heard the story of Kirk and Laura Smalley's son, Ty Field-Smalley. At age eleven, Ty took his own life after being suspended from school for retaliating against a bully who had been bullying him for over two years.
- Stomp Out Bullying
  STOMP Out Bullying (SOB) is dedicated to changing the culture for all students. It focuses on reducing and preventing bullying, cyberbullying, and other digital abuse; educates against homophobia, LGBTQIA+ discrimination, racism, and hatred; and deters violence in schools, online, and in communities across the country. SOB promotes civility, diversity, inclusion, equity, and equality, providing help for those in need and at risk of suicide, and raising awareness through peer mentoring programs in schools, public service announcements, and social media campaigns.

(*Continued*)

Table 6.2 (Continued)

- StopBullying.gov
  StopBullying.gov provides information from various government agencies on what bullying is, what cyberbullying is, who is at risk, and how you can prevent and respond to bullying. StopBullying.gov coordinates closely with the Federal Partners in Bullying Prevention Steering Committee, an interagency effort co-led by the Department of Education and the Department of Health and Human Services that works to coordinate policy, research, and communications on bullying topics.
- No Hate Speech Youth Campaign
  The No Hate Speech Movement (NHSM) is a youth campaign led by the Council of Europe Youth Department that seeks to mobilize young people to combat hate speech and promote human rights online. The NHSM website provides information about the campaign and the resources developed to prevent, counter, and produce alternative narratives to hate speech.

Learning more about contemporary hate speech scholarship

For those interested in reading more academic writings related to the topics discussed in this chapter, consider the following resources that have explored a) the complexities of regulating hate speech on the internet through legal and technological frameworks (Banks, 2010); b) approaches to detecting hate speech in online text, and mechanisms for detecting some commonly used methods of evading common "dirty word" filters (Warner & Hirschberg, 2012); and the perils of granting someone anonymity, as they are apt to behave poorly, namely with malevolence in their comments (Wulczyn, Thain, & Dixon, 2017).

Considering that many readers who access this book will be students and academic colleagues, Table 6.3 includes some further readings for those seeking contemporary scholarship addressing social media and hate speech.

Table 6.3 Further readings for those seeking contemporary scholarship addressing social media and hate speech

---

Connie Hassett-Walker. (2022). Does Brandenburg v. Ohio still hold in the social media era? Racist (and other) online hate speech and the First Amendment. *Cogent Social Sciences* 8:1. https://doi.org/10.1080/23311886.2022.2038848

Belinda Johnson, & Raelene West. (2022). Ableism versus free speech in Australia: challenging online hate speech toward people with Down syndrome. *Disability & Society* 0:0, 1–23. https://doi.org/10.1080/09687599.2022.2041402

Soudeh Ghaffari. (2022). Discourses of celebrities on Instagram: Digital femininity, self-representation and hate speech. *Critical Discourse Studies* 19:2, 161–178. https://doi.org/10.1080/17405904.2020.1839923

Rachel Keighley. (2022). Hate Hurts: Exploring the impact of online hate on LGBTQ+ Young People. *Women & Criminal Justice* 32:1–2, 29–48. https://doi.org/1 0.1080/08974454.2021.1988034

(*Continued*)

Table 6.3 (Continued)

Julia R. DeCook. (2021). r/WatchRedditDie and the politics of reddit's bans and quarantines. *Internet Histories* 0:0, 1–17. https://doi.org/10.1080/24701475.2021.199 7179

Cheuk Hang Au, Kevin K. W. Ho, & Dickson K.W. Chiu. (2021). Managing users' behaviors on open content crowdsourcing platform. *Journal of Computer Information Systems* 0:0, 1–11. https://doi.org/10.1080/08874417.2021.1983487

Katharine Sarikakis, Bruktawit Ejigu Kassa, Natascha Fenz, Sarah Goldschmitt, Julia Kasser, & Laura Nowotarski. (2021). "My haters and I": Personal and political responses to hate speech against female journalists in Austria. *Feminist Media Studies* 0:0, 1–16. https://doi.org/10.1080/14680777.2021.1979068

Andrea Waling, Anthony Lyons, Beatrice Alba, Victor Minichiello, Catherine Barrett, Mark Hughes, & Karen Fredriksen-Goldsen. (2020). Recruiting stigmatised populations and managing negative commentary via social media: A case study of recruiting older LGBTI research participants in Australia. *International Journal of Social Research Methodology* 0:0, 1–14. https://doi.org/10.1080/13645579.2020.1863545

Vittorio Lingiardi, Nicola Carone, Giovanni Semeraro, Cataldo Musto, Marilisa D'Amico, & Silvia Brena. (2020). Mapping Twitter hate speech towards social and sexual minorities: A lexicon-based approach to semantic content analysis. *Behaviour & Information Technology* 39:7, 711–721. https://doi.org/10.1080/01449 29X.2019.1607903

Edoardo Celeste. (2019). Terms of service and bills of rights: New mechanisms of constitutionalisation in the social media environment? *International Review of Law, Computers & Technology* 33:2, 122–138. https://doi.org/10.1080/13600869.2018.147 5898

Matthew Costello, Joseph Rukus, & James Hawdon. (2019). We don't like your type around here: Regional and residential differences in exposure to online hate material targeting sexuality. *Deviant Behavior* 40:3, 385–401. https://doi.org/10.1080/016396 25.2018.1426266

Leah Burch. (2018). 'You are a parasite on the productive classes': Online disablist hate speech in austere times. *Disability & Society* 33:3, 392–415. https://doi.org/10.1080/ 09687599.2017.1411250

Bad behavior will always exist

As discussed throughout this chapter, all social media users should be prepared for comments that are unpleasant. Be prepared to block, report, and move on from such vitriol. As a guide for your own behavior, we encourage you to be a kind human and engage in the use of social media with care, compassion, and support for others. To address some of the concerns outlined above, Chapter 7 will set out ethical considerations and standards of behavior for academics on social media. We strongly encourage academic institutions to incorporate ethical standards into their policy, practice, and guidelines for academic staff to help mitigate ill-effects (Figure 6.2).

Figure 6.2 Social media is better when people are kind.

Source: Photo by Ashley Whitlatch on Unsplash

7   Ethical standards for social media use by academics

As a scientist integrating ethics in my work, I'm faced with 2 camps:
1   Those that respect what I do & applaud the effort.
2   Those that avoid me due to my ethical & critical approaches.

Since when was being ethical such a bad thing?

@katherinebassil

Introduction

Navigating the landscape of social media can be a bumpy and precarious path if one proceeds without consideration of ethical consequences and professional obligations.

Social media is used by academics for different purposes, ranging from their professional teaching and research requirements to more personal needs such as networking, self-promotion, or even acquiring knowledge as part of their personal learning (Chugh et al., 2021).

While most academic institutions encourage social media use, posting public content can always carry the risk of reputational, legal, or personal damage, even unwittingly (Johannsson & Selak, 2020). However, ethical guidelines can provide a safety net for an individual's engagement in social media. They can be used either as a personal guide for decision making or at a school, faculty or at institutional level. With intentional, ethical, considered use, the benefits of social media, such as for community building, research dissemination, and networking, far outweigh negative ramifications. The use of social media offers several potential benefits in terms of improving the profile of an individual in their field of expertise, raising awareness among members of the community, and garnering the attention of the government regarding related policy issues and funding requirements (see Chapter 1 for an overview of benefits; Australian Psychological Society [APS], 2018). The following ethical guidelines have been adapted from a range of professional and regulatory bodies (e.g., APS, 2018; American Speech-Language-Hearing Association [ASHA], 2020; American Psychological Association [APA], 2021; Nursing and Midwifery Board AHPRA, 2019).

Academics who use social media for their work, uphold the standing of the institution they work for and the discipline they represent (Cabrera et al., 2017). When engaging in social media, individuals should be aware of the potential risks

DOI: 10.4324/9781003198369-10

for reputational damage – both for themselves and their institutions – and take concerted steps to mitigate this risk (Johannsson & Selak, 2020).

Academics can maintain an ethical professional presence by:

- **Ensuring all interactions on social media are courteous, professional, and respectful** (Nursing and Midwifery Board AHPRA, 2019). For example, critiquing, reviewing, or commenting on the work of others should be done in a constructive and respectful manner. Academics should also be respectful when providing professional opinions, irrespective of the extent to which their own opinions differ from those of others (APS, 2018).
- **Understanding, identifying, and taking appropriate actions related to potential conflicts of interests as they may emerge on social media** (APS, 2018). Academics should disclose potential commercial benefits or financial incentives they receive (Selwyn & Heffernan, 2021). Academics should be transparent as to whether they are endorsing content for personal or commercial gain (Selwyn & Heffernan, 2021).
- **Using evidence to support claims where possible**. Statements based on opinion or personal experience should be declared (APS, 2018). Knowledge sources should be transparent and clearly communicated.
- **Working within professional competencies**. Academics should be mindful of the limits and boundaries of their expertise (APS, 2018). For example, academics should use social media as a platform to communicate information that is relevant to their professional expertise and experience to reduce the spread of misinformation. This includes posting content which fits within their field of expertise, training, or experience (APS, 2018). In addition to this, academics should maintain appropriate levels of professional competence in the area in which they claim expertise.
- **Maintaining the privacy of others**. For example, information or images explicitly related to students, or their work should not be shared without consent. This includes stories or anecdotes. No personally identifiable information should be shared about students unless they have provided prior consent (Selwyn & Heffernan, 2021). When photos are shared, the background of the pictures should be scrutinized to ensure that personal details of others are not unintentionally shared (Nursing & Midwifery Board AHPRA, 2019).
- **Maintaining personal privacy**. Academics actively protect their own personal or sensitive information by understanding and regularly reviewing privacy settings, which can frequently change. Academics may consider holding separate personal and professional accounts.
- **Keeping a professional digital footprint by ensuring that expertise portrayed online are accurate** (Gamble & Morris, 2014). Academics should conduct regular internet searches with their name to identify erroneous information (Gamble & Morris, 2014). They should also be mindful that all content shared on the internet creates a digital history that over time can resurface. With constantly evolving social norms, the original intent or meaning of a post may change over time. This is a risk that should be considered as new content is generated.

- **Knowing that the increased popularity of digital technologies may create an additional *digital labor* for academics**. Engagement in social media for work-related purposes should remain in the scope of contractual arrangements with the academic institution (Selwyn & Heffernan, 2021). Academics who see the benefit of social media use for work-related purposes may advocate for it to be acknowledged as a legitimate service or engagement activity within the scope of their typical academic duties.

Additional resources

APA Guidelines for the Optimal Use of Social Media in Professional Psychology Practice

https://www.apa.org/about/policy/guidelines-optimal-use-social-media.pdf

This resource is intended to provide a framework for the optimal use of social media in professional psychological practice. It aims to guide psychologists in building their professional practice, increasing visibility, and optimizing communication and information dissemination through social media.

Social Media Research: A Guide to Ethics

https://www.gla.ac.uk/media/Media_487729_smxx.pdf

Social Media Research: A Guide to Ethics is an accessible and concise document that provides a guideline on the ethical use of social media in research. Its framework is designed to guide individuals in deciding the most ethical approach in doing research.

Social Media and Health Care Professionals: Benefits, Risks, and Best Practices

https://www.ncbi.nlm.nih.gov/pmc/articles/PMC4103576/

Social media is a useful tool for healthcare professionals; however, its use is also accompanied by certain risks. This article discusses the benefits, risks and best practices or guidelines in using social media for healthcare professionals.

Issues in Ethics: Ethical Use of Social Media

https://www.asha.org/practice/ethics/ethical-use-of-social-media/

This document presents issues in ethics in accordance with the Code of Ethics (2016). It provides a guide for the appropriate use of social media to prevent violations under the Code.

Social Media Ethics and Etiquette

https://www.compukol.com/social-media-ethics-and-etiquette/

The main principles of ethics and etiquette for social media – authenticity, transparency and communication – are discussed in this article.

8 The future is bright for academics

We need to embrace social media to maximize the impact of our research, especially beyond academia. Turning that paywalled technical paper into an accessible LinkedIn post or a 5 minute YouTube video helps us engage with the industry better.

@ImamPhd

Introduction

Barry Checkoway (1997) noted that

> the research university is a sleeping giant that, if awakened, can contribute mightily to the problems facing American communities. [...] Without exaggeration, there is no other societal institution with such an armada of talent and resources to focus on the problems challenging American communities.
>
> (p. 327)

Could social media offer an opportunity to wake the sleeping giant? Has social media had a major impact in the restructuring of the core values and missions of academic institutions in general?

The reality of academic work has traditionally been limited to teaching, research, and service (sometimes referred to as engagement), with teaching and research typically prioritized in most institutions. Academic work can be slowed down by processes like peer review (Allen et al., 2020) which can contribute to a lag time between scholarly theory and research and what can be used in practice (Kolars, 2011). Yet, despite being learning centers, a key role of academic institutions is not only to educate the population while generating new knowledge (Perkmann et al., 2013) but also to address the economic and social needs of society, a purpose for which many institutions were originally established (Bond & Paterson, 2005). An academic's work in service and engagement can be particularly important for translating research into social impact, but more work is needed in this space for academic institutions to fully encourage and value social impact. Unless social

DOI: 10.4324/9781003198369-11

impact is explicitly articulated in academic performance standards alongside traditional academic metrics of scholarship, words like impact and engagement become nothing more than buzz words.

In recent years, under the influence of globalization and the internet, there has been a seismic shift in the way academics communicate to non-scholarly audiences, and social media has offered a new platform for academics characterized by immediacy and autonomy. Never has there been a time where academics could freely publish work and share ideas. Of course, caution must be taken. Peer-review offers a fundamentally important role in ensuring checks and balances occur with research that is disseminated to mitigate harm to the general public, although peer-review processes aren't necessarily flawless. It is critical that ethical standards, as presented in Chapter 7, are adhered to while simultaneously acknowledging the benefits of social media channels. There is a need to find ways in which academics and academic institutions engaging in social media work (and effective science communication) can have their work valued and respected.

There are four potential benefits for a future where academic social media engagement is encouraged:

1   The diminishing notion of ivory towers
2   A stronger focus on social impact, research translation, and countering misinformation
3   Building global networks, international connections, and industry collaborations
4   Contributing to a market economy

The diminishing notion of ivory towers and shifting priorities for academic institutions

Notions of academics working in a closed environment, or so-called ivory towers, are quickly becoming an artifact of the past. The internet and specifically social media have enabled academics to bridge connections with academics in other disciplines as well as students in a way that has never been seen before. This has allowed academic institutions to contribute to social development in new and innovative ways (Compagnucci & Spigarelli, 2020; Urdari et al., 2017) and break through the shackles of disciplinary boundaries or the usual barriers that preclude connection with important stakeholders.

Academic institutions have several stakeholders such as students, staff, and funders, and since effective communication between an institution and its stakeholders is critical (Mogaji, 2019), the use of online platforms provides another means through which this can be achieved (Farinloye et al., 2020). For instance, with social media being extremely popular among many students, academic institutions offer students a natural and organic means through which they can easily interact with a virtual community via groups or profiles on social networking sites (Assimakopoulos et al., 2017).

Lara Tate, a graduate student in educational psychology, reflects on her experiences of using social media to stay connected during lockdowns (Figure 8.1).

Figure 8.1 Social media can improve the learning experiences of students.
Source: Photo by Brooke Cagle on Unsplash

CASE STUDY: Social media as another way to connect

By Lara Tate, Monash University

I have pretty much completed my whole master's course online given the university closures due to COVID-19. Although this has physically disconnected myself from Monash grounds, I can honestly say I have never felt more connected to my fellow peers in the course and faculty staff. As a cohort we have a Monash Master of Educational and Developmental Psychology 2020 group on Facebook as well as a combined group with the Professional Psychology students. Within these groups we ask course-related questions, express our thoughts and opinions, facilitate group discussions, and share resources and updates. I believe that this has really promoted a great level of togetherness, collaboration, and support and has brought us closer as a cohort. Using Facebook has enabled me to have informal online discussions and learn a lot from my fellow peers.

Another platform which has also been incredibly useful is WhatsApp. Within this platform I have a thesis group chat with my supervisor and fellow peers in the thesis group. In this chat we share resources related to our thesis and check in with each other. It's been such a great casual way to chat about our thesis and stay connected. My supervisor and myself also communicate through WhatsApp. I have found that this is so much easier than email as it's more efficient and personable. We can both send each other voice messages through the app which I believe aids communication, and I have found that it has really helped with my learning and understanding by listening to my supervisor as opposed to writing emails back and forth. Whenever I had thesis-related questions, my supervisor promptly replied through a voice message in WhatsApp explaining what I needed to do. I found this incredibly useful as person-ally I find verbal explanations a lot easier to understand compared to written. I wish that I had these groups in my other courses at a different university as I have been able to see first-hand the benefits of using online platforms the past two years.

A stronger focus on social impact, research translation, and countering misinformation

In addition to diminishing ivory towers, social media can also exert a certain level of influence or change on members of society and offer benefits aiding social impact. Because of this, academic institutions are gradually reconsidering how they address societal needs through social media platforms. Some academic institutions have used social media platforms to interact or engage in discussions with the general public on issues that are relevant to them (e.g., to educate on matters per-taining to public health or to create townhall-style discussions) (Giustini et al., 2018; Huber et al., 2020; Mendoza-Herrera et al., 2020).

During the COVID-19 pandemic, academic institutions also used social media to inform people about the virus and offer public education on how to prevent its spread. This was one way academics played a powerful role in mitigating misinfor-mation. The term *infodemic*, coined by the World Health Organization, refers to the dangers associated with the spread of misinformation, especially during disease outbreaks (Cinelli et al., 2020). Although this phenomenon has always existed in one way or another, social media has amplified its effects in respect to the speed in which information is shared and the volume of people who now rely on social media to consume news (Zarocostas, 2020). After the onset of COVID-19, when people's social media use increased due to quarantine and lockdown measures, social media users became vulnerable to misinformation. While social media was used by most to keep in touch with others and stay informed about the prevailing situation (Abbas et al., 2021), myths circulated about the origins of the coronavirus and the efficacy and safety of vaccines. There were several unfortunate cases where

Figure 8.2 The infodemic might be here to stay, but academics on social media have a role to play in offering a credible and reliable voice to combat misinformation.

Source: Photo by Jorge Franganillo on Unsplash

individuals learnt about '*cures*' for COVID which led to deaths. The infodemic reached unprecedented levels, prompting researchers to widely investigate its harmful impact as evident from the large number of available articles on this topic (Bridgman et al., 2021; Cinelli et al., 2020; Melki et al., 2021; Zhang et al., 2021).

A central concern with an infodemic is that it can influence members of the public and promote a lack of trust in government and authorities, curbing efforts to manage a particular situation (Adekoya & Fasae, 2021; Lillian, 2021). It is virtually impossible to avoid the spread of false information on social media. However, academics can help mitigate this issue by helping to increase and spread more reliable and accurate communication (Melki et al., 2021; Lillian, 2021). Academics can actively assist in dispelling myths associated with either disinformation (deliberately made false news) or misinformation (questionable information due to improperly verified news) through conferences, interviews, or even through their online presence on social media (Chugh et al., 2021; Johannsson & Selak, 2020; Lillian, 2021). The future of academic work may require a stronger shift from the traditional *educator* or *researcher* roles in the academy, to *advisor* or public figure. Although it is worth noting that on social media, there are presently no means of verifying the identity of those claiming to be experts in their fields. No mechanisms exist especially for academics to be officially verified, unlike celebrities, politicians, influencers, and sporting identities. Thus, fake profiles are a concern and can be another way misinformation is spread, and while there are measures to detect fake profiles (Romanov et al., 2017), they are not always effective. Despite these drawbacks and constraints amidst the ongoing infodemic, future academics may find themselves considering a calling or moral duty to engage in social media to counteract misinformation (Figure 8.2).

Building global networks, international connections, and industry collaborations

Translating research outcomes into practice can also be made possible through online social networking sites through the facilitation of collaboration (Long et al., 2015). Social media platforms, especially those designed for academics, highlight the research interests, research impact, and other useful information about their users. As a result, such platforms encourage previously unacquainted researchers with similar interests to connect in a way that would otherwise have only been possible during physical meetings or conferences. The remarkable increase in the number of international collaborations during the past few years (Hoang et al., 2019) highlights the value of social media for this purpose. Social media provides a platform for connection and communication, irrespective of a researcher's location. Collaboration is not limited to academics, and hence, by bringing together both academics and non-academic organizations, social media provides an opportunity for research outcomes produced by academia to be implemented by non-academic counterparts. Ultimately, this assists in research translation and fulfills academic institutions' contributions to society (Compagnucci & Spigarelli, 2020; Perkmann et al., 2013; Rauchfleisch et al., 2021).

University–industry collaborations are often regarded as essential for the progress of both research and developments in industry. While academic institutions are focused on generating and disseminating new knowledge, industries apply that knowledge to produce goods, services, or other outcomes that can benefit society (Pourdeyhimi, 2020). While the mission and purpose of industry versus the academy as standalone institutions may seem unrelated (Gulbrandsen & Smeby, 2005), the collaboration between the two is mutually beneficial for both parties. To a large extent, academic institutions rely on external funds to support their projects and fund the salaries of researchers (Gläser & Velarde, 2018). Collaboration with industry offers sources of income that ultimately supplement or even sustain the activities of academic institutions. Funding from industry sources has become even more important following COVID-19 where sources of competitive funding have been reduced or diminished. Some academics have turned their attention to industry funding to meet Key Performance Indicators (KPIs), and academic institutions acknowledge the importance of industry relations in order to exist in the future. But there are numerous advantages of such collaborations, beyond funding alone. For instance, industry may have access to new technologies needed for research or they may have resources for training and development (Wang et al., 2020). Also, because many researchers strive to have applied and practical implications for their research, industry collaboration assists with social impact due to the potential for commercialization, patenting, or licensing of research products that may emerge (Perkmann et al., 2013). Due to the many benefits of such collaborations, it is not surprising that academic institutions are now being increasingly funded by industry (Gulbrandsen & Smeby, 2005).

Social media can help academics make their research more visible to industry. Troy Heffernan has received multiple opportunities due to his presence on social media (Figure 8.3).

Figure 8.3 Social media can strengthen reach and impact of traditional research.
Source: Photo by Kelsey Knight on Unsplash

CASE STUDY: "You want people to know your research"

By Dr. Troy Heffernan, La Trobe University (@troyheff)

One of the academic papers I'm most proud of has been downloaded 20,000 times from the journal's website. However, I wrote about the paper on Twitter and LinkedIn, and thanks to the available metrics on these platforms, I know these tweets and posts have been seen and interacted with by over 5,000,000 users. This alone blows my mind as to what is possible with social media. That five million people have seen my name, and got a small glimpse into what my work is about would happen no other way other than with social media. I know that most of those five million people probably don't want to know more about me or my work, but some do. And it's because of social media that people have seen my work because they were scrolling on their phone, not because they were looking for papers about a specific topic in a specific journal.

The paper is about helping marginalised people in higher education; a sector reserved for the privileged few for centuries, and one that sometimes still has trouble breaking that cycle in the twenty-first century. So the paper is a topic relevant to a global sector, and it was social media that brought my research to a global audience. Since the paper was published, I have worked with universities, research companies, and government departments in countries all over the world. Time and time again though, the first email I receive from someone keen to know more, asking me to do a presentation, or asking if I'm available for consultancy work, says 'I saw people talking about your paper on Twitter' or 'Someone sent me a link to your paper on LinkedIn'.

I know it has been social media that has started these conversations, but it's also been social media that got the ball rolling on people knowing my research and knowing what I've done. Social media started the initial flurry of interest and work, but now it's the fact I've done that work the leads to new inquiries. Increasingly my emails begin 'I know you worked with such and such university', or 'I saw your presentation for this or that government department'.

This is perhaps one of the greatest objectives of anyone working in the higher education or social justice fields. You want people to know your research, but you also want people to know that you (and your research) can make policy and practical changes that help improve the lives of others. I had a solid body of research, and I now have a strong portfolio of international work and impact, and I use these to be more persuasive in getting more people to take larger steps in enhancing their institution's, department's, or company's equity practices. However, at the core of the changes I have been able to make, are the first steps that happened thanks to the global audience of social media.

Contributing to a market economy

Disrupted by COVID-19 and the impact of a decline in student numbers, academic institutions around the world have set new priorities for attracting prospective students. As a result, social media has been used by academic institutions and universities to deliver targeted marketing strategies (Chen & DiVall, 2018; Farinloye et al., 2020; Motta & Barbosa, 2018; Peruta & Shields, 2018). While these strategies are often mediated by marketing professionals (Motta & Barbosa, 2018), academics play a role in *marketing* their institutions also, even if only by simply using social media platforms.

While vicariously promoting your employer might not be the most motivating factor for academics' social media use, working for a thriving academic institution might be. An institution with a good public reputation may attract more students and funds, which can keep academics employed, foster research, drive new developments and theories, generate new knowledge, and nurture a new generation of academics.

A final thought

We have had a chance to examine some of the benefits and pitfalls of social media use. By implementing strategies that mitigate harmful online experiences and considering ethical standards and practice, academics are in a good place to harness the more positive side of social media for their work. As discussed in this chapter, it is almost certain that social media will be an important part of academic work in the future, particularly for academics who wish to have broad reach and dissemination of their work. The next chapter (Chapter 9) covers some of the most frequently asked questions about social media that might not have been covered so far in this book.

9 Frequently asked questions about social media use in academia

I'm not sure why some academics seem scared of social. It's a tool, like others. It's a great mechanism to share interesting findings, but of course, if everything is pay-walled to mostly academics, that can be limiting. I guess it depends on your goals

@JonathanDunnett

FAQ questions	Answers
What is social media?	Social media allows individuals to communicate, network, and share information through various web-based platforms.
What are social networking sites?	Social networking sites, also known as social media sites, allow members to keep track of the activities of their connections, exchange messages, upload photos, join groups based on interests, and engage with users.
What are the top 10 social media apps?	As of 2022, the top 10 social media sites and platforms are Facebook, YouTube, WhatsApp, Instagram, TikTok, Snapchat, Reddit, Pinterest, Twitter, and LinkedIn.
What social media apps are specifically aimed at academics?	There are certain platforms such as ResearchGate and Academia. edu which combine the benefits of social networking sites and the requirements of academia.
What are the uses of social networking sites?	Social networking sites allow users to create profiles, post photos and videos, share professional achievements, and connect with others. For an academic, this can provide an easy way to stay connected with colleagues, disseminate research findings, engage in work-orientated activities (e.g., interacting with students, online lectures, celebrating successes, and prompting discussions), find opportunities for collaboration, host virtual meetings, and attend virtual conferences.
Why should I join social media?	Social networking sites offer many benefits, including helping you stay connected with peers and finding new ones, with the opportunity to set up international/interdisciplinary collaborations. It is also possible to share research-related information with colleagues on different platforms (e.g., research proposals, published papers), thus getting more visibility while getting advice from more senior academics. And there are plenty of online communities where you can meet others interested in similar topics for constructive discussions or even for holding virtual conferences/meetings. Some online forums even allow you to express your expert opinions or share relevant content (e.g., on a "hot" topic currently in the news) to a lay audience to inform, educate, or guide decision-making processes.

(Continued)

DOI: 10.4324/9781003198369-12

FAQ questions	Answers
What additional benefits will academic social networking sites provide me with?	In addition to networking opportunities, most academic-based social networking sites offer services that are tailored to academics. Much like an academic CV, many sites provide opportunities to list of all your publications (or a link to your professional website or profile), information on your research expertise, major contributions, and awards. It is also possible to keep track of citation counts (often a criterion used to measure academic impact) and even to use "citation alerts" to inform you whenever your work has been cited by other authors. Finally, since these platforms are mostly limited to academics, it is easier to link up with fellow researchers with similar interests for future collaborations.
What information is necessary when joining or creating a social media account?	The information needed will depend on the individual social networking site you plan to join. Generally, they ask for name, birthdate, location, and email address. Those specifically aimed at academics may even request information on your academic position, research interests, contributions (e.g., list of publications), major awards, etc. There is usually also an option to keep this information private.
Why should I use social media platform?	Facebook offers many benefits to users who log onto its website regularly. Users gain access to news feeds, photos, videos, and other content shared by friends, colleagues, and acquaintances. For academics, news feeds can be used as a source of information to keep yourself up-to-date with current research. Academic content can be posted, allowing others, including other academics, to comment or engage. There are opportunities to join closed groups where members share information and ideas.
When should I use social media platform?	Use Facebook when you feel comfortable doing so. Don't let anyone pressure you into joining just because an institution or individual requires you to do so. Post things that interest you or that you think will interest others, whether it's news articles, photos, or videos. However, be wary about posting anything personal. Many academics have separate personal and professional profiles or pages. Understanding privacy and visibility settings can be immensely beneficial for using the site effectively.
What should I know before joining a social networking site?	Social networking sites are becoming an integral part of an academic's life. Facebook, Twitter, and LinkedIn are the most popular social networking sites today. While each site offers its own unique benefits, there are several things to consider before joining any network. First, decide whether you want to join one specific site or multiple ones. Second, determine who you would like to connect with (e.g., peers, colleagues, collaborators, funding agencies, etc.). Third, be clear on the objectives of using the social networking sites (personal vs. professional use). Professional objectives will most likely focus on research dissemination and promoting your work. Finally, choose between public and private networks. Public networks offer access to anyone, providing more visibility to the content that you post. However, privacy settings may limit visibility. Private networks require users to request permission to view profiles.

FAQ questions	Answers
How often should I update my status?	Social networking sites like Facebook and Twitter allow users to share information through updates called "status messages." These updates appear on other members' news feeds when they log onto the site. There are times when updating one's status too frequently might seem excessive or inappropriate. However, if people are not engaging with your updates, then they'll generally be shown in your updates less over time. However, do consider updating it anytime you feel that shared information would serve your academic goals or be of interest to other members and fellow researchers (e.g., sharing a link to your newly published article, updating your status with news about a breakthrough discovery in your field of interest, available funding opportunities, an upcoming conference, etc.).
How do I get verified?	Social media sites like Facebook, Twitter, and LinkedIn allow users to connect with friends and colleagues through online profiles. Users typically create an account on one or several social networks before connecting with others.
	A verified account is verified by the respective platform as being a true and accurate account of the person represented. On Twitter and Instagram there is currently not a verification category for academics, but this is likely to change in the future, at least for Twitter.
Why do I need to get verified?	Verification helps ensure that your identity is established. In addition, verification may improve your experience on the network by, for example, giving more credibility to the content of your posts and reducing copy-cat accounts.
What are the differences between LinkedIn, Instagram, Facebook, and Twitter?	While each social media platform offers its own benefits, there are several similarities among the four most popular platforms. All allow users to post photos, videos, text messages, and other content. They also offer similar functions, including sharing posts with friends/colleagues or the public in general, liking others' updates, commenting on others' posts, and following others' updates. Each site allows users to connect with contacts through email addresses, phone numbers, or even physical locations. And while many sites require an account to see content, LinkedIn does not. Instagram does not allow direct links in posts. Twitter limits posts to 280 characters whereas the other sites allow longer posts.
Which social media should I use as a professional account?	Social media platforms provide an opportunity to market yourself professionally by showcasing your achievements to a wider audience than an individual would be able to reach without social media. In addition, social media sites allow you to connect with other scholars who share similar research interests, hence providing unprecedented opportunities to establish collaborations. Many academic institutions and universities now recommend academics to maintain profiles on LinkedIn, Facebook, and Twitter, among others, to promote themselves or their works, with an online presence for the purpose of things like research translation and dissemination considered a desirable component of the academic role (e.g., emphasized in promotion applications).

(Continued)

FAQ questions	Answers
I'm already very busy, why should I spend time on social media?	We all have a set amount of time that we can work, so it's not a question of time but rather how you spend and prioritize your time. The benefits of social media make it worthwhile to prioritize your time on these platforms.
I'm an early career academic with no publications, so what do I share?	While sharing publications is one kind of thing to post on social media, there's much more that can be posted in terms of the research process. This includes interesting articles, research tools that you're using, or even sharing the experience of being an early career academic.
What's an algorithm?	In computer science, an algorithm is a collection of rules that describes how a set of data acts. In social media, an algorithm has a vital role in determining what posts people see in their feeds. While there is debate online about what can influence the algorithm, most advice generally states that users should post quality content regularly and engage frequently in the content posted by others (e.g., by liking, saving, sharing content, etc.).

Be curious

In order to use social media successfully, for many academics, there will be an ongoing learning curve as platforms and technologies change and develop over time.

Stay curious and ask questions.

At the end of the day, there is ultimately only *one thing* you need to know about using social media successfully and this is covered in Chapter 10.

10 The final word on using social media successfully

Be kind, always.

DOI: 10.4324/9781003198369-13

References

Abbas, J., Wang, D., Su, Z., & Ziapour, A. (2021). The role of social media in the advent of COVID-19 pandemic: Crisis management, mental health challenges and implications. *Risk Management and Healthcare Policy*, *14*, 1917–1937. https://doi.org/10.2147/RMHP.S284313

Adekoya, C. O., & Fasae, J. K. (2021). Social media and the spread of COVID-19 infodemic. *Global Knowledge, Memory and Communication*, *71*(3). https://doi.org/10.1108/GKMC-11-2020-0165

Allen, K. A. (2019). What is the actual impact of measuring academic notions of impact? *The Educational and Developmental Psychologist*, *36*(2), 33–34. https://doi.org/10.1017/edp.2019.16

Allen, K. A., Donoghue, G., Pahlevansharif, S., Jimerson, S. R., & Hattie, J. A. C. (2020). Addressing academic rejection: Recommendations for reform. *Journal of University Teaching & Learning Practice*, *17*(5), Article 19.

Allen, K. A., Ryan, T., Gray, D. L., McInerney, D., & Waters, L. (2014). Social media use and social connectedness in adolescents: The positives and the potential pitfalls. *The Australian Educational and Developmental Psychologist*, *31*(1), 18–31. https://doi.org/10.1017/edp.2014.2

American Psychological Association [APA]. (2021). *APA Guidelines for the optimal use of social media in professional psychology practice.* https://www.apa.org/about/policy/guidelines-optimal-use-social-media.pdf

American Speech-Language-Hearing Association [ASHA]. (2020). *Issues in ethics: Ethical use of social media.* https://www.asha.org/practice/ethics/ethical-use-of-social-media/

Ansari, J. A. N., & Khan, N. A. (2020). Exploring the role of social media in collaborative learning the new domain of learning. *Smart Learning Environments*, 7(1). https://doi.org/10.1186/s40561-020-00118-7

Arshad, M., & Akram, M. S. (2018). Social media adoption by the academic community: Theoretical insights and empirical evidence from developing countries. *The International Review of Research in Open and Distributed Learning*, *19*(3). https://doi.org/10.19173/irrodl.v19i3.3500

Asmi, N. A., & Margam, M. (2018). Academic social networking sites for researchers in Central Universities of Delhi: A study of ResearchGate and Academia. *Global Knowledge, Memory and Communication*, *67*(1/2), 91–108. https://doi.org/10.1108/GKMC-01-2017-0004

Assimakopoulos, C., Antoniadis, I., Kayas, O. G., & Dvizac, D. (2017). Effective social media marketing strategy: Facebook as an opportunity for universities. *International Journal of Retail & Distribution Management*, *45*(5). https://doi.org/10.1108/IJRDM-11-2016-0211

122   *References*

Australian Psychological Society [APS]. (2018). *Ethical guidelines for working with and in the media.* https://psychology.org.au/getmedia/c70b2b8c-44dc-4e4e-a0bc-08fb7c03e72a/ Ethical-guideline-media.pdf

Bahadori, M., Raadabadi, M., Ravangard, R., & Mahaki, B. (2016). The barriers to the application of the research findings from the nurses' perspective: A case study in a teaching hospital. *Journal of Education and Health Promotion, 5,* Article 14. https://doi.org/10.4103/ 2277-9531.184553

Balakrishnan, V., & Loo, H. S. (2013). Social Media in e-Learning: An empirical analysis among students and academicians. *GSTF Journal on Computing, 2*(4), 145–149.

Banks, J. (2010). Regulating hate speech online. *International Review of Law, Computers & Technology, 24*(3), 233–239. https://doi.org/10.1080/13600869.2010.522323

Bauer, M. S., Damschroder, L., Hagedorn, H., Smith, J., & Kilbourne, A. M. (2015). An introduction to implementation science for the non-specialist. *BMC Psychology, 3,* Article 32. https://doi.org/10.1186/s40359-015-0089-9

Bauer, M. S., & Kirchner, J. (2020). Implementation science: What is it and why should I care? *Psychiatry Research, 283,* Article 112376. https://doi.org/10.1016/j.psychres. 2019.04.025

Bennet, A., & Bennet, D. (2008). *Knowledge mobilization in the social sciences and humanities: Moving from research to action.* MQI Press.

Blannin, J., Kidman, G., Tan, S. C., Tan, D., & Dewi, F. (2021, November 4). *How South-East Asian students learn in lockdowns.* Monash University. https://www.monash.edu/ education/teachspace/articles/how-south-east-asian-students-learn-in-lockdowns

Boateng, R. O., & Amankwaa, A. (2016). The impact of social media on student academic life in higher education. *Global Journal of Human-Social Science: G Linguistics & Education, 16*(4), 1–7.

Bonaiuti, G. (2015). Academic social networks: How the web is changing our way to make and communicate researches. *REM – Research on Education and Media, 7*(2), 3–14. https:// doi.org/10.1515/rem-2015-0010

Bond, R., & Paterson, L. (2005). Coming down from the ivory tower? Academics' civic and economic engagement with the community. *Oxford Review of Education, 31*(3), 331–351. https://doi.org/10.1080/03054980500221934

Bray, R. (2000). *SPIN works.* Independent Media Institute.

Brems, C., Temmerman, M., Graham, T., & Broersma, M. (2016). Personal branding on Twitter: How employed and freelance journalists stage themselves on social media. *Digital Journalism, 5*(4), 443–459. https://doi.org/10.1080/21670811.2016.1176534

Bridgman, A., Merkley, E., Zhilin, O., Loewen, P. J., Owen, T., & Ruths, D. (2021). Infodemic pathways: Evaluating the role that traditional and social media play in cross-national information transfer. *Frontiers in Political Science.* https://doi.org/10.3389/fpubh.2021. 610623

Britton, B., Jackson, C., & Wade, J. (2019). The reward and risk of social media for academics. *Nature Reviews Chemistry, 3*(8), 459–461. https://doi.org/10.1038/s41570-019-0121-3

Cabrera, D., Vartabedian, B. S., Spinner, R. J., Jordan, B. L., Aase, L. A., & Timimi, F. K. (2017). More than likes and tweets: Creating social media portfolios for academic promotion and tenure. *Journal of Graduate Medical Education, 9*(4), 421–425. https://doi.org/10.4300/ JGME-D-17-00171.1

Carmel, R. G., & Paul, M. W. (2015). Mentoring and coaching in academia: Reflections on a mentoring/coaching relationship. *Policy Futures in Education, 13*(4), 479–491. https:// doi.org/10.1177/1478210315578562

Carrigan, M. (2019). *Social media for academics.* Sage.

Chang, Y. (2021). Academic impact of articles by practitioners in the field of library and information science. *College & Research Libraries, 82*(1), 59–74. https://doi.org/10.5860/crl.82.1.59

Chen, E., & DiVall, M. (2018). Social media as an engagement tool for schools and colleges of pharmacy. *American Journal of Pharmaceutical Education, 82*(4), Article 6562. https://doi.org/10.5688/ajpe6562

Chugh, R., Grose, R., & Macht, S. A. (2021). Social media usage by higher education academics: A scoping review of the literature. *Education and Information Technologies, 26*(1), 983–999. https://doi.org/10.1007/s10639-020-10288-z

Cinelli, M., Quattrociocchi, W., Galeazzi, A., Valensise, C. M., Brugnoli, E., Schmidt, A. L., Zola, P., Zollo, F., & Scala, A. (2020). The COVID-19 social media infodemic. *Scientific Reports, 10*(1), 16598. https://doi.org/10.1038/s41598-020-73510-5

Cohn, C. (2010, March 20). *Social media ethics and etiquette.* CompuKol Communications. https://www.compukol.com/social-media-ethics-and-etiquette/

Coleman, J. (2022, January 4). *The social media video statistics marketers need to know for 2022.* Sprout Social. https://sproutsocial.com/insights/social-media-video-statistics/

Compagnucci, L., & Spigarelli, F. (2020). The third mission of the university: A systematic literature review on potentials and constraints. *Technological Forecasting and Social Change, 161*, Article 120284. https://doi.org/10.1016/j.techfore.2020.120284

D'Alessandro, S., Miles, M., Martínez-López, F. J., Anaya-Sánchez, R., Esteban-Millat, I., & Torrez-Meruvia, H. (2020). Promote or perish? A brief note on academic social networking sites and academic reputation. *Journal of Marketing Management, 36*(5–6), 405–411. https://doi.org/10.1080/0267257X.2019.1697104

Davison, R. M., & Bjørn-Andersen, N. (2019). Do we care about the societal impact of our research? The tyranny of the H-index and new value-oriented research directions. *Information Systems Journal, 29*(5), 989–993. https://doi.org/10.1111/isj.12259

DeCastro, R., Sambuco, D., Ubel, P. A., Stewart, A., & Jagsi, R. (2013). Mentor networks in academic medicine: Moving beyond a dyadic conception of mentoring for junior faculty researchers. *Academic Medicine: Journal of the Association of American Medical Colleges, 88*(4), 488–496. https://doi.org/10.1097/ACM.0b013e318285d302

Dijkstra, S., Kok, G., Ledford, J. G., Sandalova, E., & Stevelink, R. (2018). Possibilities and pitfalls of social media for translational medicine. *Frontiers in Medicine, 5*, Article 345. https://doi.org/10.3389/fmed.2018.00345

Duffy, B. E., & Pooley, J. D. (2017). "Facebook for academics": The convergence of self-branding and soocial media logic on Academia.edu. *Social Media + Society, 3*(1), 1–11. https://doi.org/10.1177/2056305117696523

Elliott, S. A., Dyson, M. P., Wilkes, G. V., Zimmermann, G. L., Chambers, C. T., Wittmeier, K. D., Russell, D. J., Scott, S. D., Thomson, D., & Hartling, L. (2020). Considerations for health researchers using social media for knowledge translation: Multiple case study. *Journal of Medical Internet Research, 22*(7), Article e15121. https://doi.org/10.2196/15121

Farinloye, T., Wayne, T., Mogaji, E., & Watat, J. K. (2020). Social media for universities' strategic communication. In E. Mogaji, F. Maringe, & R. E. Hinson (Eds.), *Strategic Marketing of Higher Education in Africa.* Routledge. https://doi.org/10.4324/9780429320934-8

Fecher, B., & Hebing, M. (2021). How do researchers approach societal impact? *PloS One, 16*(7), Article e0254006. https://doi.org/10.1371/journal.pone.0254006

Fileborn, B. (2016). Participant recruitment in an online era: A reflection on ethics and identity. *Research Ethics, 12*(2), 97–115. https://doi.org/10.1177/1747016115604150

Finch, T., O'Hanlon, N., & Dudley, S. P. (2017). Tweeting birds: Online mentions predict future citations in ornithology. *Royal Society Open Science, 4*(11), Article 171371. https://doi.org/10.1098/rsos.171371

Forbes, D. (2017). Professional online presence and learning networks: Educating for ethical use of social media. *International Review of Research in Open and Distributed Learning, 18*(7), 175–190. https://doi.org/10.19173/irrodl.v18i7.2826

Fryirs, K. A., Brierley, G. J., & Dixon, T. (2019). Engaging with research impact assessment for an environmental science case study. *Nature Communications, 10*(1), Article 4542. https://doi.org/10.1038/s41467-019-12020-z

Gamble, N., & Morris, Z. (2014). *Ethical and competent practice in the online age*. InPsych. https://psychology.org.au/inpsych/2014/june/gramble

Gelinas, L., Pierce, R., Winkler, S., Cohen, I. G., Lynch, H. F., & Bierer, B. E. (2017). Using social media as a research recruitment tool: Ethical issues and recommendations. *The American Journal of Bioethics, 17*(3), 3–14. https://doi.org/10.1080/15265161.2016.1276644

Giustini, D. M., Ali, S. M., Fraser, M., & Boulos, M. N. K. (2018). Effective uses of social media in public health and medicine: A systematic review of systematic reviews. *Online Journal of Public Health Informatics, 10*(2), Article e215. https://doi.org/10.5210/ojphi.v10i2.8270

Gläser, J., Velarde, K. S. (2018). Changing funding arrangements and the production of scientific knowledge: Introduction to the special issue. *Minerva, 56*(1), 1–10. https://doi.org/10.1007/s11024-018-9344-6

Gorbatov, S., Khapova, S. N., & Lysova, E. I. (2018). Personal branding: Interdisciplinary systematic review and research agenda. *Frontiers in Psychology, 9*, Article 2238. https://doi.org/10.3389/fpsyg.2018.02238

Gorbatov, S., Khapova, S. N., & Lysova, E. I. (2019). Get noticed to get ahead: The impact of personal branding on career success. *Frontiers in Psychology, 10*, Article 2662. https://doi.org/10.3389/fpsyg.2019.02662

Green, L. W. (2014). Closing the chasm between research and practice: Evidence of and for change. *Health Promotion Journal of Australia, 25*(1), 25–29. https://doi.org/10.1021/jp506374m

Gulbrandsen, M., & Smeby, J.-C. (2005). Industry funding and university professors' research performance. *Research Policy, 34*(6), 932–950. https://doi.org/10.1016/j.respol.2005.05.004

Haynes, L., Adams, S. L., & Boss, J. M. (2008). Mentoring and networking: How to make it work. *Nature Immunology, 9*(1), 3–5. https://doi.org/10.1038/ni0108-3

Heffernan, A., Bright, D., Kim, M., Longmuir, F., & Magyar, B. (2022). 'I cannot sustain the workload and the emotional toll': Reasons behind Australian teachers' intentions to leave the profession. *Australian Journal of Education*. https://doi.org/10.1177/00049441221086654

Heffernan, T. (2020). Academic networks and career trajectory: 'There's no career in academia without networks'. *Higher Education Research & Development*, 1–14. https://doi.org/10.1080/07294360.2020.1799948

Hoang, D. T., Nguyen, N. T., Tran, V. C., & Hwang, D. (2019). Research collaboration model in academic social networks. *Enterprise Information Systems, 13*(7–8), 1023–1045. https://doi.org/10.1080/17517575.2018.1556812

Holmberg, K., Bowman, S., Bowman, T., Didegah, F., & Kortelainen, T. (2019). What is societal impact and where do altmetrics fit into the equation? *Journal of Altmetrics, 2*(1), Article 6. http://doi.org/10.29024/joa.21

Huang, S., Martin, L. J., Yeh, C. H., Chin, A., Murray, H., Sanderson, W. B., Mohindra, R., Chan, T. M., & Thoma, B. (2018). The effect of an infographic promotion on research dissemination and readership: A randomized controlled trial. *Canadian Journal of Emergency Medicine, 20*(6), 826–833. https://doi.org/10.1017/cem.2018.436

Huber, J., Woods, T., Fushi, A., Duong, M. T., Eidelman, A. S., Zalal, A. R., Urquhart, O., Colangelo, E., Quinn, S., & Carrasco-Labra, A. (2020). Social media research strategy to understand clinician and public perception of health care messages. *JDR Clinical & Translational Research*, *5*(1), 71–81. https://doi.org/10.1177/2380084419849439

Jaakola, M. (2017). The scholarly use of social media: How to make the most of it? *Nordicom-Information*, *39*(1), 59–71.

Jabeur, L. B., Tamine, L., & Boughanem, M. (2010). A social model for literature access: Towards a weighted social network of authors. *Adaptivity, Personalization and Fusion of Heterogeneous Information*, 32–39. https://link.springer.com/content/pdf/10.1007%2 F978-3-030-98438-0.pdf

Jackson, V. A., Palepu, A., Szalacha, L., Caswell, C., Carr, P. L., & Inui, T. (2003). "Having the right chemistry": A qualitative study of mentoring in academic medicine. *Academic Medicine*, *78*, 328–334. https://doi.org/10.1097/00001888-200303000-00020

Jacobson, J. (2020). You are a brand: Social media managers' personal branding and "the future audience". *Journal of Product & Brand Management*, *29*(6), 715–727. https://doi.org/10.1108/JPBM-03-2019-2299

Johannsson, H., & Selak, T. (2020). Dissemination of medical publications on social media – is it the new standard? *Anaesthesia*, *75*(2), 155–157. https://doi.org/10.1111/anae.14780

Jordan, K. (2019). From social networks to publishing platforms: A review of the history and scholarship of academic social network sites. *Frontiers in Digital Humanities*, *6*, Article 5. https://doi.org/10.3389/fdigh.2019.00005

Jordan, K., & Weller, M. (2018). Academics and social networking sites: Benefits, problems and tensions in professional engagement with online networking. *Journal of Interactive Media in Education*, *2018*(1), Article 1. https://doi.org/10.5334/jime.448

Karaduman, I. (2013). The effect of social media on personal branding efforts of top level executives. *Procedia – Social and Behavioral Sciences*, *99*(2013), 465–473. https://doi.org/10.1016/j.sbspro.2013.10.515

Klar, S., Krupnikov, Y., Ryan, J. B., Searles, K., & Shmargad, Y. (2020). Using social media to promote academic research: Identifying the benefits of twitter for sharing academic work. *PLoS One*, *15*(4), Article e0229446. https://doi.org/10.1371/journal.pone.0229446

Kolars, J. C. (2011). Taking down 'the ivory tower': Leveraging academia for better health outcomes in Uganda. *BMC International Health and Human Rights*, *11*(S1), 1–3. https://doi.org/10.1186/1472-698X-11-S1-S1

Lair, D. J., Sullivan, K., & Cheney, G. (2005). Marketization and the recasting of the professional self. *Management Communication Quarterly*, *18*(3), 307–343. https://doi.org/10.1177/0893318904270744

Lillian, S. (2021, April 2). Higher education has a role in curbing disinformation. *University World News Africa Edition*. https://www.universityworldnews.com/post.php?story= 20210401070014617

Liu, Y. C., Hung, Y. Y., & Gunawan, J. (2018). A model to explore personal brand in social networks. In *iiWAS2018: Proceedings of the 20th International Conference on Information Integration and Web-Based Applications & Services* (pp. 306–309). https://doi.org/10.1145/3282373.3282380

Long, J. C., Hibbert, P., & Braithwaite, J. (2015). Structuring successful collaboration: A longitudinal social network analysis of a translational research network. *Implementation Science*, *11*, Article 19. https://doi.org/10.1186/s13012-016-0381-y

Lupton, D. (2014). *'Feeling better connected': Academics' use of social media*. News & Media Research Centre, University of Canberra.

Malcolm, J., & Zukas, M. (2009). Making a mess of academic work: Experience, purpose and identity. *Teaching in Higher Education*, *14*(5), 495–506. https://doi.org/10.1080/13562510903186659

Maloney, S., Tunnecliff, J., Morgan, P., Gaida, J. E., Clearihan, L., Sadasivan, S., Davies, D., Ganesh, S., Mohanty, P., Weiner, J., Reynolds, J., & Ilic, D. (2015). Translating evidence into practice via social media: A mixed-methods study. *Journal of Medical Internet Research*, *17*(10), Article e4763. https://doi.org/10.2196/jmir.4763

Melki, J., Tamim, H., Hadid, D., Makki, M., El Amine, J., & Hitti, E. (2021). Mitigating infodemics: The relationship between news exposure and trust and belief in COVID-19 fake news and social media spreading. *PLoS One 16*(6), Article e0252830. https://doi.org/10.1371/journal.pone.0252830

Mendoza-Herrera, K., Valero-Morales, I., Ocampo-Granados, M. E., Reyes-Morales, H., Arce-Amaré, F., & Barquera, S. (2020). An overview of social media use in the field of public health nutrition: Benefits, scope, limitations, and a Latin American experience. *Preventing Chronic Disease*, *17*, Article E76. https://doi.org/10.5888/pcd17.200047

Merga, M. K., Roni, S. M., & Mason, S. (2020). Should Google Scholar be used for benchmarking against the professoriate in education? *Scientometrics*, *125*, 2505–2522. https://doi.org/10.1007/s11192-020-03691-3

Miller, A. (2016, September 16). York University fires faculty member after alleged anti-Semitic social media posts. *Global News*. https://globalnews.ca/news/2945561/york-university-fires-faculty-member-after-alleged-anti-semitic-social-media-posts/

Mogaji, E. (2019). Strategic stakeholder communications on Twitter by UK universities. *Research Agenda Working Papers*, *2019*(8), 104–119.

Motta, J., & Barbosa, M. (2018). Social media as a marketing tool for European and North American universities and colleges. *Journal of Intercultural Management*, *10*(3), 125–154. https://doi.org/10.2478/joim-2018-0020

Newport, C. (2019). *Digital minimalism: Choosing a focused life in a noisy world*. Portfolio (Penguin Random House). https://www.calnewport.com/books/digital-minimalism/

Nursing and Midwifery Board Ahpra. (2019). *New social media guide*. https://www.nursingmidwiferyboard.gov.au/News/2019-11-11-Social-media-guide.aspx

Park, J., Williams, A. S., & Son, S. (2020). Social media as a personal branding tool: A qualitative study of student-athletes' perceptions and behaviors. *Journal of Athlete Development and Experience*, *2*(1), 51–68. https://doi.org/10.25035/jade.02.01.04

Parry, D. A., Davidson, B. I., Sewall, C. J., Fisher, J. T., Mieczkowski, H., & Quintana, D. S. (2021). A systematic review and meta-analysis of discrepancies between logged and self-reported digital media use. *Nature Human Behaviour*, *5*(11), 1535–1547. https://doi.org/10.1038/s41562-021-01117-5

Pawlak, K. M., Siau, K., Bilal, M., Donet, J. A., Charabaty, A., & Bollipo, S. (2021). Young GI angle #Twitter2Paper: Taking an idea from Twitter to paper. *United European Gastroenterology Journal*, *9*(1), 129–132. https://doi.org/10.1002/ueg2.12053

Penfield, T., Baker, M. J., Scoble, R., & Wykes, M. C. (2013). Assessment, evaluations, and definitions of research impact: A review. *Research Evaluation*, *23*(1), 21–32. https://doi.org/10.1093/reseval/rvt021

Perkmann, M., Tartari, V., McKelvey, M., Autio, E., Broström, A., D'Este, P., Fini, R., Geuna, A., Grimaldi, R., Hughes, A., Krabel, S., Kitson, M., Llerena, P., Lissoni, F., Salter, A., & Sobrero, M. (2013). Academic engagement and commercialisation: A review of the literature on university–industry relations. *Research Policy*, *42*(2), 423–442. https://doi.org/10.1016/j.respol.2012.09.007

Peruta, A., & Shields, A. B. (2018). Marketing your university on social media: A content analysis of Facebook post types and formats. *Journal of Marketing for Higher Education*, *28*(2), 175–191. https://doi.org/10.1080/08841241.2018.1442896

Petrucă, I. (2016). Personal branding through social media. *International Journal of Communication Research*, *6*(4), 389–392.

Pourdeyhimi, B. (2020). University research funding: Why does industry funding continue to be a small portion of university research, and how can we change the paradigm? *Industry and Higher Education*, *35*(3), 150–158. https://doi.org/10.1177/0950422220962286

Puljak, L. (2016). Using social media for knowledge translation, promotion of evidence-based medicine and high -quality information on health. *Journal of Evidence-Based Medicine*, *9*(1), 4–7. https://doi.org/10.1111/jebm.12175

Quintana, D. S., & Doan, N. T. (2016). Twitter article mentions and citations: An exploratory analysis of publications in the American Journal of Psychiatry. *American Journal of Psychiatry*, *173*(2), 194. https://doi.org/10.1176/appi.ajp.2015.15101341

Rauchfleisch, A., Schäfer, M. S., & Siegen, D. (2021). Beyond the ivory tower: Measuring and explaining academic engagement with journalists, politicians and industry representatives among Swiss professors. *PLoS One*, *16*(5), Article e0251051. https://doi.org/10.1371/journal.pone.0251051

Robinson, O., & Spring, M. (2020, March 19). Coronavirus: How bad information goes viral. *BBC News*. https://www.bbc.com/news/blogs-trending-51931394

Romanov, A., Semenov, A., Mazhelis, O., & Veijalainen, J. (2017). Detection of fake profiles in social media: Literature review. In *Proceedings of the 13th International Conference on Web Information Systems and Technologies* (pp. 363–369). SCITEPRESS. https://doi.org/10.5220/0006362103630369

Ryan, J. (2020, February 17). *Top 5 Milkshake Ducks*. Lifehacker. https://www.lifehacker.com.au/2020/02/top-5-milkshake-ducks/

Ryan, T., Allen, K. A., Gray, D. L., & McInerney, D. M. (2017). How social are social media? A review of online social behaviour and connectedness. *Journal of Relationships Research*, *8*(e8), 1–8. https://doi.org/10.1017/jrr.2017.13

Saad, N. H. M., & Yaacob, Z. (2021). Building a personal brand as a CEO: A case study of Vivy Yusof, the cofounder of FashionValet and the dUCk Group. *SAGE Open*, *11*(3). https://doi.org/10.1177/21582440211030274

Sandalova, E., Ledford, J. G., Baskaran, M., & Dijkstra, S. (2019). Translational medicine in the era of social media: A survey of scientific and clinical communities. *Frontiers in Medicine*, *6*, Article 152. https://doi.org/10.3389/fmed.2019.00152

Selwyn, N., & Heffernan, A. (2021). Teachers' work with digital technologies. In K. A. Allen, A. Reupert, & L. Oades (Eds.), *Building Better Schools with Evidence-based Policy* (pp. 131–138). Routledge. https://doi.org/10.4324/9781003025955-18

Smit, J. P., & Hessels, L. K. (2021). The production of scientific and societal value in research evaluation: A review of societal impact assessment methods. *Research Evaluation*, *30*(3), 323–335. https://doi.org/10.1093/reseval/rvab002

Smith, D., Schlaepfer, P., Major, K., Dyble, M., Page, A. E., Thompson, J., Chaudhary, N., Salali, G. D., Mace, R., Astete, L., Ngales, M., Vinicius, L., & Migliano, A. B. (2017). Cooperation and the evolution of hunter-gatherer storytelling. *Nature Communications*, *8*(1), Article 1853. https://doi.org/10.1038/s41467-017-02036-8

Smith, R. (2001). Measuring the social impact of research. *British Medical Journal*, *323*(7312), 528. https://doi.org/10.1136/bmj.323.7312.528

Smith, Z. L., Chiang, A. L., Bowman, D., & Wallace, M. B. (2019). Longitudinal relationship between social media activity and article citations in the Journal Gastrointestinal Endoscopy. *Gastrointestinal Endoscopy*, *90*(1), 77–83. https://doi.org/10.1016/j.gie.2019.03.028

Straus, S. E., Chatur, F., & Taylor, M. (2009). Issues in the mentor-mentee relationship in academic medicine: A qualitative study. *Academic Medicine, 84*, 135–139. https://doi.org/10.1097/ACM.0b013e31819301ab

Streeter, J. (2014). Networking in academia. *EMBO Reports, 15*(11), 1109–1112. https://doi.org/10.15252/embr.201439626

Sutherland, K., Terton, U., Davis, C., Driver, C., & Visser, I. (2020). Academic perspectives and approaches to social media use in higher education: A pilot study. International *Journal of Teaching and Learning in Higher Education, 32*(1), 1–12.

Taylor, H. L. (1997). No more ivory towers: Connecting the research university to the community. *Journal of Planning Literature, 11*(3), 327–332. https://doi.org/10.1177/088854122970110030

Thoma, B., Mohindra, R., Artz, J. D., & Chan, T. M. (2015). CJEM and the changing landscape of medical education and knowledge translation. *Canadian Journal of Emergency Medicine, 17*(2), 184–187. https://doi.org/10.1017/cem.2015.16

Townsend, L., & Wallace, C. (2016). *Social media research: A guide to ethics.* University of Aberdeen. https://www.gla.ac.uk/media/Media_487729_smxx.pdf

Urdari, C., Farcas, T.V., & Tiron-Tudor, A. (2017). Assessing the legitimacy of HEIs' contributions to society: The perspective of international rankings. *Sustainability Accounting, Management and Policy Journal, 8*(2), 191–215.

Utz, S., & Breuer, J. (2019). The relationship between networking, LinkedIn use, and retrieving informational benefits. *Cyberpsychology, Behavior and Social Networking, 22*(3), 180–185. https://doi.org/10.1089/cyber.2018.0294

van Eperen, L., & Marincola, F. M. (2011). How scientists use social media to communicate their research. *Journal of Translational Medicine, 9*(1), Article 199. https://doi.org/10.1186/1479-5876-9-199

Vanichvasin, P. (2021). Effects of visual communication on memory enhancement of Thai undergraduate students, Kasetsart University. *Higher Education Studies, 11*(1), 34–41.

Vasquez, E. F. K., & Bastidas, C. E. C. (2015). Academic social networking sites: A comparative analysis of their services and tools. In *iConference 2015 Proceedings.* https://www.ideals.illinois.edu/handle/2142/73715

Ventola, C. L. (2014). Social media and health care professionals: Benefits, risks, and best practices. *Pharmacy and Therapeutics, 39*(7), 491–499.

Wang, Y., Chen, Y., Li, W., Wang, T., Guo, L., Li-Ying, J., & Huang, J. (2020). Funding research in universities: Do government resources act as a complement or substitute to industry funding? *Economic Research-Ekonomska Istrazivanja, 33*(1), 1377–1393. https://doi.org/10.1080/1331677X.2020.1746189

Warner, W., & Hirschberg, J. (2012). Detecting hate speech on the world wide web. In *Proceedings of the Second Workshop on Language in Social Media* (pp. 19–26). Association for Computational Linguistics. https://aclanthology.org/W12-2103/

Weiss, K. (2020). The social media sandwich: How to communicate your research on social media. *Rethinking Research.* https://www.insidehighered.com/blogs/rethinking-research/social-media-sandwich-how-communicate-your-research-social-media-1

Wulczyn, E., Thain, N., & Dixon, L. (2017). Ex machina: Personal attacks seen at scale. In *Proceedings of the 26th International Conference on World Wide Web* (pp. 1391–1399). International World Wide Web Conferences Steering Committee. https://doi.org/10.1145/3038912.3052591

Yadav, A., Phillips, M. M., Lundeberg, M. A., Koehler, M. J., Hilden, K., & Dirkin, K. H. (2011). If a picture is worth a thousand words is video worth a million? Differences in affective and cognitive processing of video and text cases. *Journal of Computing in Higher Education, 23*(1), 15–37. https://doi.org/10.1007/s12528-011-9042-y

Zarocostas, J. (2020). How to fight an infodemic. *The Lancet, 395*(10225), 676. https://doi.org/10.1016/S0140-6736(20)30461-X

Zhang, D., & Earp, B. E. (2020). Correlation between social media posts and academic citations of orthopaedic research. *JAAOS: Global Research and Reviews, 4*(9). https://doi.org/10.5435/JAAOSGlobal-D-20-00151

Zhang, S., Pian, W., Ma, F., Ni, Z., & Liu, Y. (2021). Characterizing the COVID-19 infodemic on Chinese social media: Exploratory study. *JMIR Public Health Surveillance, 7*(2), Article e26090. https://doi.org/10.2196/26090

Zientek, L. R., Werner, J. M., Campuzano, M. V., & Nimon, K. (2018). The use of google scholar for research and research dissemination. *New Horizons in Adult Education and Human Resource Development, 30*(1), 39–46. https://doi.org/10.1002/nha3.20209

Index

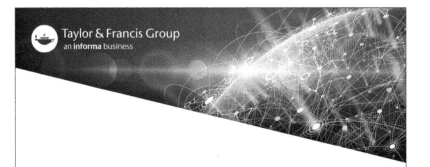

For Product Safety Concerns and Information please contact our EU
representative GPSR@taylorandfrancis.com
Taylor & Francis Verlag GmbH, Kaufingerstraße 24, 80331 München, Germany

www.ingramcontent.com/pod-product-compliance
Ingram Content Group UK Ltd.
Pitfield, Milton Keynes, MK11 3LW, UK
UKHW021455080625
459435UK00012B/520